Let Me Count The Ways In Which We Have All Been Deceived

By

Boyd B. McNiel

Let Me Count The Ways In Which We Have All Been Deceived

Let Me Count The Ways In Which We Have All Been Deceived

Published 12/30/2017

By
Boyd B. McNiel.
All rights are reserved.
Printed in the United States of America

No part of this book may be reproduced in any manner what-so-ever without the written permission from the Author.

Please write to:
Boyd B. McNiel
P.O. Box 624
Pea Ridge, Arkansas 72751
Or e-mail me at: bmcniel@centurytel.net
Or telephone me at: (479)-877-9732

Table Of Contents

I	Knowledge Of The Truth	7
II	Boxes Of Evidence	8
III	The Three Monkeys	10
IV	One Simple Truth	11
V	The Truth	12
VI	The Renewing Of The Mind	14
VII	The Straight And Narrow Gate	15
VII	Meet The Author	16
1	Establishing A Foundation	19
2	Right *Versus* Wrong	23
3	Inherited Lies *Versus* The Traditions Of Men	31
4	What's In A Name?	36
5	Interpretation	56
6	Where Did The; "J" Come From?	59
7	Speaking the Names Of False Deities	62
8	What Time Do You Have	72
9	When Is Your Next Holi-day?	98
10	Where Did The Deception Begin?	106
11	Break Down Their Images	118
12	The Central Theme Of The Scriptures	125
13	Circumcision On The 8th Day	132
14	They Have Broken The Everlasting Covenant	135
15	What Are The Real Commandments Of Ehyeh?	154

Let Me Count The Ways In Which We Have All Been Deceived

16   The Cutting And Pasting Of The Scriptures 162
17   North 171
18   The Battle Of Armageddon 176
19   Immanuel 186
20   The Holy Spirit – The Set-Apart Mind-Set 191
21   Adultery 198
22   30 Pieces Of Silver 200
23   The Litmus Test 203
24   The Switch 206
25   Burnt Offerings And Sacrifices, (Slaughtering's) 210
26   The Word 215
27   The Greatest Con The World Has Ever Known 218
28   The Pass-Over Verses The Passover 221
29   Yeshua's True Birthday 224
30   The False Pen Of The Scribes 227
31   They Have Changed The Ordinances 231
32   Ehyeh's 364 Day Calendar 235
33   2 Esdras 240
34   The Last Nail 244
35   Index Of Words From Pagan Origins 247
36   Appendix 249
37   The Book Of Oahspe 254
38   The Conclusion 262
39   From The Author 265

Knowledge Of The Truth

Proverbs 25:2 tells us, *"It is the majesty of Ehyeh to conceal things: but it is also the honor of kings to search those things out."*

2 Timothy 2:4 tells us, Ehyeh desires that, *"all of mankind be saved and come to the knowledge of The Truth."*

In other words, *"It is the majesty of Ehyeh to conceal things: but it is also the honor of kings to search those things out. So that all of mankind be saved and come to the knowledge of The Truth."*

Let Me Count The Ways In Which We Have All Been Deceived

Boxes of Evidence

The reason several answers may be given is quite simple, and should be obvious. Different evidence exists to support each different answer! This might best be illustrated by the following diagram which I call my "Boxes of Evidence."

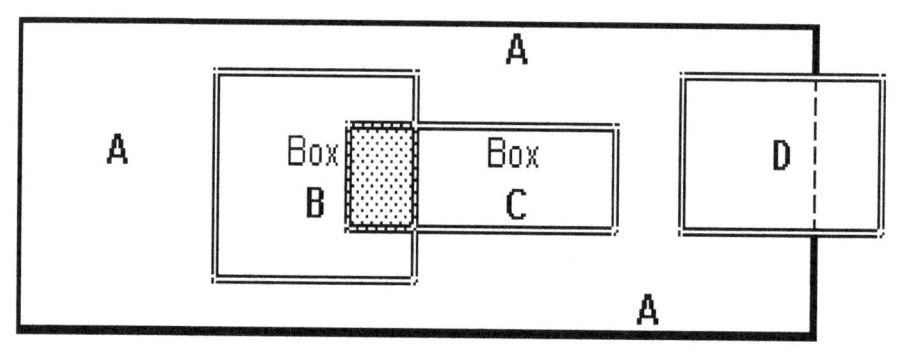

In the preceding diagram, the largest of the four boxes (area "A") represents the whole body of evidence that may exist on any particular subject. The three smaller boxes within area "A" (areas "B," "C," and "D,") represent a small portion of that whole body of evidence, to which scholars/experts "B," "C," and "D" have been respectively exposed. People are exposed to different areas of the whole body of evidence through their study and environment.

Since people are naturally exposed to different areas of the whole body of evidence, they may disagree with each other. But each of these "scholars" **think** that the evidence they have been exposed to represents the whole of area "A." They **think** they have 100% of the evidence on any particular subject, and since *they* have it, and you disagree; you must be completely delusional!

Let Me Count The Ways In Which We Have All Been Deceived

The 3 Monkeys

Most of the monkey figurines that you find shows each monkey covering his own eyes and his own ears and his own mouth. These Three Monkeys on the front cover of this book are quite unique, in that all three of them are each working hand in hand to deceive themselves and each other.

These Three Monkeys represent the blind Pharisees, the false scribes and all of the stiff-necked individuals who only want to have their ears tickled and erroneously believe that they already have all The Truth that they need to know.

Let Me Count The Ways In Which We Have All Been Deceived

One Simple Truth

One Simple Truth can be used as the foundation for a mountain of lies, but when one digs down deep into that mountain of lies and brings that **One Simple Truth** out and places it on the top of that mountain of lies, that entire mountain of lies will crumble under the weight of that **One Simple Truth**.

There is nothing more devastating to a structure of lies than the exposure of that **One Simple Truth** upon which the structure of lies was established on, because the shock waves from the disclosure of that **One Simple Truth** will continue to reverberate throughout the earth for generations to come, awakening even those individuals who had no desire to be awakened to that **One Simple Truth**.

By: Delamer Duverus

Let Me Count The Ways In Which We Have All Been Deceived

The Truth

- **Proverbs 16:16** says, *How much better is it to get wisdom than gold!*
- **John 8:32** says, *"You shall know "The Truth" and "The Truth" shall make you free."*
- The people who discover gold can become wealthy. But the individual who discovers **"The Truth"** is wealthy beyond measure. **"The Truth"** is by far more precious than gold.
- **"The Truth"** is like Pandora's Box. Once you have discovered **"The Truth"** it can never be unlearned.
- **"The Truth"** will always be the **"The Truth"** regardless of someone's lack of understanding, disbelief, or ignorance.
- **"The Truth"** stands alone by itself. It does not need anyone to agree with it for it to be **"The Truth." "The Truth"** is **"The Truth"** whether you believe it or not.
- **"The Truth"** exists; only lies are invented.

- **"The Truth"** is like the sun. You can shut it out for a time, but it isn't going away.
- Denying **"The Truth"** doesn't change the facts.
- Never apologize for telling **"The Truth."**
- **"The Truth"** will set you free, but first it will make you miserable.

The Renewing Of The Mind

Romans 12:1-2 says, *"I plead with you brothers and sisters, by the mercies of Ehyeh, that you present your bodies as a living offering, which is set-apart and acceptable unto Ehyeh, which is your minimum reasonable service. And do not be conformed to this world: 2 But you must become transformed by **the renewing of your mind**, so that you may prove that which is the good and acceptable perfect will of the Most High Creator."*

The most important thing is that; "You must have a **renewing of your mind**."

The Straight And Narrow Gate

Matthew 7:14 tells us that, *"The gate is broad and the path which leads to destruction is wide, and there are many who go in through it: But you must enter in by the straight gate: Because the straight gate is the narrow gate, and it is the path which leads to life and there are few who find the narrow gate."*

- In Other Words -

The gate leading to the path of destruction is broad and wide and the greatest majority of you will enter in through that gate of destruction. But you need to enter through the straight and narrow gate which is the path which leads to everlasting life.

Are you one of those very few individuals who are actually seeking to find that straight and narrow gate which leads to everlasting life?

Meet The Author

My mother sent me to Catholic Catechism when I was six years old, and I asked the priest why we were supposed to pray to Mary. He told me, "That is what we do."

When I got home, I told my dad what the priest had said, and my dad told my mom that I did not have to go back to Catechism if I did not want to go because the man had not answered my question very well. I have never liked pacifying answers. I never went back.

When I was seven years old I got into a fight because another boy said that my mom was a liar for telling me that there was a Santa Clause and an Easter Bunny. I lost that fight in two ways that day. When I got home my mom told me **"The Truth"**. I was so devastated that I cried about it for a week.

Later on, as I grew up, I went to quite a few different religious assemblies seeking to learn **"The Truth"**, but I always felt that I was not hearing the whole truth. As a result, I quit going to any of them for a long time.

Let Me Count The Ways In Which We Have All Been Deceived

When I was in the Navy, I was stationed on the Aircraft Carrier, the USS Nimitz for a couple of years. When we were at sea the USS Nimitz had approximately 6,000 men on board.

I was continually in conflict with my superiors because I would not adapt or conform to military protocol. As a result, I was sent to Captain's Mast four separate times for several minor infractions and I was eventually discharged because I would not always salute the officers or say, "Sir" to them.

In the end, Captain Ilg and I had a private conversation in his office. He told me that of all the men on his ship, he knew that I alone would be willing to tell him **"The Truth"**, even if it was not what he wanted to hear. He told me that he recognized that characteristic in me the very first time that he had met me. Captain Ilg said that I would probably always feel like I was fighting an uphill battle with everyone else because practically everyone else had been taught not to question things that they had been taught. He said that it was those same men who were **"being led as sheep to the slaughter"**.

The last thing that Captain Ilg told me as I was getting ready to leave his office was for me to never allow others to make me think or feel that I was wrong, because, he said, I was "probably" the only one in the right. This was the first time anyone had ever explained all of this to me. I felt a heavy weight lift off of my shoulders. It was because of that 45-minute conversation with Captain Ilg that I feel that I should present this book to you. If the Captain had not explained all of this to me about myself, I probably would never have understood that I do not perceive most things the same way that most others do.

Let Me Count The Ways In Which We Have All Been Deceived

I took a metal machine shop class when I was in the Navy and I learned to machine things with very close tolerances within, plus or minus a thousandth of an inch.

After I got out of the Navy, I worked in construction where I learned that everything has to be 'absolutely straight, plumb, level and square'. With that mental frame of mind and philosophy I always had a problem with all of these various religious assemblies teaching that; "You can come just as you are, and you do not have to change."

Years later, when I got married to my wife, she told me that she thought that we should start going to a church. I told her that it was fine with me, but, if we were going to do that, we were not going to go just to socialize. I told her that if we found that the church was not preaching and teaching what the scriptures were saying, we would not continue going. I told her that we would follow **"The Truth"** wherever it led us.

When I discovered that the Scripture tells us the whole world, (except for the elect) would be deceived and that the entry gate is very narrow, I began searching for that narrow gate. I knew in my soul that I was not hearing The Truth from the (Pharisees) preachers. So, I started reading the Scriptures for myself and I began to see a lot of anomalies that have led me to many of the conclusions which I have presented to you in this book.

Now that you know a little bit about me and where I am coming from, I invite you to read along, and we will discover many of the false teachings that have been taught to both you and me by the hypocritical scribes and the false Pharisees. Please try and keep a running count. There are nearly three hundred deceptions revealed in this book alone. Many of these lies are obvious once someone has pointed them out to you.

1
Establishing A Foundation

People often say that "hindsight is 20/20." Having 20/20 vision is considered to be equivalent to having perfect vision. This statement alludes to the fact that we should learn from our previous mistakes. More to the point is, "I wish that I would have known then what I know now."

The same thing could be said about learning something new from a textbook. Have you ever read a book that had additional details in the latter chapters which you wish the author would have told you about in the earlier chapters - especially, when these additional details turn out to be a complete game changer?

In the following pages of this book, I intend to share some of what I have personally discovered about the Most High Creator and the Scriptures. Many of the things which I intend to share with you will more than likely upset you. Some of these things will actually make you extremely mad. As a friend of mine likes to say, "The Truth will set you free, but first it will #iss you off." The reason that **"The Truth"** will upset you so much is because you will want to know why you have been lied to for such a long time.

Let Me Count The Ways In Which We Have All Been Deceived

The following are four separate excerpts from the book; **The Gospel of Truth** which I believe are very applicable to what I intend to share with you:

- *"He who is ignorant is in need and what he lacks is great, since he lacks that which will make him perfect".*

- *"Therefore, if one has knowledge, he is from above. If he is called, he hears, he answers, and he turns to him who is calling to him and ascends to him"... .*

- *"Having knowledge, he does the will of the one who called him, he wishes to be pleasing to him and he receives rest."*

- *"As in the case of the ignorance of a person, when he comes to have knowledge, his ignorance vanishes of itself, just as the darkness vanishes when light appears, so also the deficiency vanishes in the perfection."*

When it comes to the knowledge of the Creator and His instructions, we should not be learning just to become smarter than the next individual. Knowledge is a very powerful tool. Knowledge without wisdom, however, is worthless. Knowledge will make an individual accountable. When an individual discovers a particular new truth, that newfound truth can become a two-edged sword. To understand what I am referring to about a two-edged sword you must understand that a sword is a weapon for defense as well as a weapon for killing.

To give you another example: Water can also be considered a two-edged sword. If you get enough water to drink during a drought, you will survive. But, if you get too much water during a flood you might drown. Embracing newfound knowledge may permit you to live. Ignoring that newfound knowledge can be detrimental to your health.

This book that you have in your hands has been somewhat difficult for me to write because I am revealing a lot of new truths to you that you may find hard to accept. I want you, the reader, to read this and learn this new knowledge without offending you or your previously established beliefs. This can be somewhat hard to accomplish. As another associate of mine likes to say, "The main obstacle to truth is the belief that you already have it!"

I know from personal experience that there have been many times when someone has shared some totally new information with me and my first response back to them was that what they had said was completely wrong. It was not until sometime later on in time that I came to the conclusion that what they had previously said to me had actually been correct. It turned out that my initial conclusion was incorrect. It turns out that later on when I heard this same thing, from someone else; I had to reconsider that what that first individual had said to me might actually have some truthful merit. **Proverbs 18:13** tells us, *"An individual who makes a final decision about anything without listening to all of the facts is a fool and this decision will bring shame to that individual."* Every one of us has done this same thing a time or two and we have all learned to regret our initial decisions.

In order for me to share many of the things that we have been deceived about, I will be going back and forth all over the Scriptures to reveal to you what I am referring to. **Isaiah 28:9-10** asks the question; *"Whom shall He* (the Most High Creator) *teach knowledge? And whom shall He make to understand doctrine? Them that are weaned off of the milk and drawn away from the breasts. 10 For precept* *must be upon precept and precept upon precept; line upon line and line upon line; here a little and there a little."*

It is my intention to make this as simple to comprehend as I possibly can, but some of this may still be somewhat hard to follow. I also want this to come across as being as lighthearted as I can make it – as opposed to being strict and dogmatic – but when it is all said and done, this information is all still the difference between life and death.

(Note): If an author or someone else ever tells you that he or she has all of the answers, then run as fast as you can. No one has it all figured out. The things that you learn from this book are just the foundational groundwork for what you can learn on your own. We are always learning. Even while I was researching and writing this particular book, I discovered additional knowledge.

newfound knowledge may permit you to live. Ignoring that newfound knowledge can be detrimental to your health.

This book that you have in your hands has been somewhat difficult for me to write because I am revealing a lot of new truths to you that you may find hard to accept. I want you, the reader, to read this and learn this new knowledge without offending you or your previously established beliefs. This can be somewhat hard to accomplish. As another associate of mine likes to say, "The main obstacle to truth is the belief that you already have it!"

I know from personal experience that there have been many times when someone has shared some totally new information with me and my first response back to them was that what they had said was completely wrong. It was not until sometime later on in time that I came to the conclusion that what they had previously said to me had actually been correct. It turned out that my initial conclusion was incorrect. It turns out that later on when I heard this same thing, from someone else; I had to reconsider that what that first individual had said to me might actually have some truthful merit. **Proverbs 18:13** tells us, *"An individual who makes a final decision about anything without listening to all of the facts is a fool and this decision will bring shame to that individual."* Every one of us has done this same thing a time or two and we have all learned to regret our initial decisions.

In order for me to share many of the things that we have been deceived about, I will be going back and forth all over the Scriptures to reveal to you what I am referring to. **Isaiah 28:9-10** asks the question; *"Whom shall He* (the Most High Creator) *teach knowledge? And whom shall He make to understand doctrine? Them that are weaned off of the milk and drawn away from the breasts. 10 For precept* *must be upon precept and precept upon precept; line upon line and line upon line; here a little and there a little."*

It is my intention to make this as simple to comprehend as I possibly can, but some of this may still be somewhat hard to follow. I also want this to come across as being as lighthearted as I can make it – as opposed to being strict and dogmatic – but when it is all said and done, this information is all still the difference between life and death.

(Note): **If an author or someone else ever tells you that he or she has all of the answers, then run as fast as you can. No one has it all figured out. The things that you learn from this book are just the foundational groundwork for what you can learn on your own. We are always learning. Even while I was researching and writing this particular book, I discovered additional knowledge.**

2
Right Versus Wrong (Truth Versus Error)

There are always two sides to every coin. We cannot have it both ways. Only one side of the coin is exposed at a time. If heads is good, then that means that tails is bad. We must always choose the good. So, when you see that the Scriptures have a story written in two completely different ways, then you must conclude that something is erroneous. One way or the other is in error. There is also the chance that both stories are just that; "stories."

Now I know what you were just thinking as you were reading that last paragraph. You were thinking that this could not possibly be true, because we have all been taught that the Scriptures (the words of the Almighty Creator) are infallible. **2 Timothy 3:16** tells us that; "*All Scripture is given by inspiration of the Sovereign and is profitable for doctrine, for reproof, for correction and for instruction in righteousness.*" Well, am I correct? Is that what you were thinking? That was the first verse that I always went to when someone tried to tell me something new.

Another unique thing that another associate always makes a point of saying is, "Do not check your brains at the door." Just because the Scriptures says something, does not necessarily mean that it is completely true.

If **2 Timothy 3:16** is correct, then what do we do with all of the following verses of Scripture:

- In **Matthew 23:13, 14, 15, 16, 23, 25, 27, 29**; the Messiah was speaking to the priests and writers of the Scriptures. He said, "*Woe unto you scribes and you Pharisees, you hypocrites*" eight separate times! He was implying that the scribes and the Pharisees have completely corrupted and manipulated the Scriptures.

- **Matthew 24:24** says, "*For there shall arise false Messiahs and false prophets and they shall show great signs and wonders; insomuch that, if it were possible, they shall deceive the very elect.*"

- **Yeremiah 8:8** says, "*How do you say, we are wise, and the instruction of the Almighty is with us? Lo, certainly he made it in vain; the pen of the scribes is in vain.*"

- **Yeremiah 16:19** says, "*O Sovereign, my strength and my fortress and my refuge in the day of affliction, the heathen nations shall come to you from the ends of the earth and shall say, surely our fathers have inherited lies, vanity and things wherein there is no profit.*"

- **Revelation 18:3-4** says, "*for the (heathen) nations have drunk of the wine of the wrath of her fornication and the kings of the earth have committed fornication with her and the merchants of the earth have become* rich through the abundance of _her_ delicacies. 4 And I heard another voice from heaven, saying, **Come out of her, my people,** so that you be not partakers of _her_ sins and so that you receive not of her plagues."

- **Hosea 4:6** tells us, "_My people are destroyed for lack of knowledge:_ because you **(priests)** have rejected knowledge, I will also reject you, so that you shall be no priest to me: seeing as you have forgotten the law of your Sovereign, I will also forget your descendants."

- **2 Thessalonians 2:9-12** tells us, "_the wicked one will come with the power of Satan and perform all kinds of false miracles and wonders and use every kind of wicked deceit on those who will perish. They will perish because they did not welcome and love The Truth so as to be saved._ And so, the Sovereign sends the power of error to work in them so that they believe what is false. _The result is that all who have not believed The Truth_, but have taken pleasure in sin, _will be condemned._"

- **Colossians 2:8** says, "_Beware lest any man deceive you through philosophy and vain deceit, after the tradition of men, after the rudiments of the world and not after the Messiah._"

- **Proverbs 14:12** says, "_There is a way which seems right unto a man, but the end thereof is the ways of death._"

- **Proverbs 25:2** says, "*It is the majesty of the Sovereign to conceal a thing: but it is <u>the honor of kings to search out a matter</u>.*"
- **John 5:39** says, "*Search the Scriptures; for in them <u>you think you have eternal life</u>: and they are they which testify of me.*"
- **Judges 17:6** says, "*In those days there was no king in Israel, but <u>every man did that which was right in his own eyes</u>.*"
- **Isaiah 43:27** says, "*Your first ancestors sinned, and your interpreters* (scribes) *have transgressed against me.*"

2 Timothy 3:16 says, "*<u>All Scripture</u>*"... According to most versions of Scripture, there are 66 books that make up the words of the Sovereign. Question: Have you ever heard of the **Apocrypha**? The original **1611 Version** of the **King James Version of Scripture** has <u>14</u> additional books which were taken out of the modern-day **King James Version of Scripture**. Could it be possible that the assembly leaders (the Pharisees) did not want you to read these 14 additional books that make up the **Apocrypha**?

> **(Note):** I do not know about you, but I do not believe it should be the Pharisees' decision to make as to whether or not I read those additional books. I believe that I should be the one who decides if these books are authentic or not. By removing these books from your version of Scripture, the Pharisees have taken away your individual ability to decide for yourself whether or not the information in these additional books is important and relevant or not.

Let Me Count The Ways In Which We Have All Been Deceived

Below is a list of the 14 books of the Apocrypha:
- Wisdom of Solomon (The Book of Wisdom)
- Tobit
- I Maccabees
- II Maccabees
- Judith
- Baruch
- Letter of Yeremiah
- I Esdras
- II Esdras – Very informative; this is profound.
- Prayer of Azariah
- Suzanna
- Bel & the Dragon
- Prayer of Manasseh
- Sirach (Ecclesiasticus) – I highly recommend this book.

In addition to these 14 books from the **Apocrypha**, there are still yet even more books. The **Book of Yasher** is mentioned two separate times and the epistle from Laodicea is also mentioned.

- **Yoshua 10:13** says, *"Is not this written in the Book of Jasher"?*
- **1 Samuel 1:18** says, *"It is written in the Book of Jasher"?*
- **Colossians 4:16** says, *"To read the epistle from Laodicea."*

I highly recommend that you get the following books and start your own personal scriptural library.

- **The Book of Yasher**
- **The Gospel of Thomas**
- **The Book of Yubilees**
- **The Book of Enoch**
- **The Book of Sirach**
- **The Gospel of the Birth of Mary**
- **The Book of the Gospel of the Twelve**

The Appendix at the back of this book has a list of about 50% of the books that maybe should have been included in the Scriptures.

The Scriptures also mention several books that have not been discovered as of yet:

- **1 Kings 11:41** mentions the book of the Acts of Solomon.
- **1 Kings 14:19** mentions the book of the chronicles of the kings of Israel (Yeshurun).
- **1 Kings 14:29** mentions the book of the chronicles of the kings of Judah.
- **1 Chronicles 9:1** mentions the book of the kings of Israel and Judah ...
- **2 Chronicles 12:15** mentions the book of Shemaiah the prophet and of Iddo the seer ...
- **2 Chronicles 20:34** mentions the book of Jehu the son of Hanani ...
- **Esther 10:2** mentions the book of the chronicles of the kings of Media and Persia.
- **Nahum 1:1** mentions the book of the vision of Nahum the Elkoshite.

- **Luke 3:4** mentions the book of the words of Esaias the prophet ...

As I stated, these additional books are not included in your regular Scriptures, but when I am referring to any of these writings I always say; "**The Scriptures**." As I have already implied, the best way to deceive the masses is to not even allow the people to have access to these additional books. The next best way to deceive the people would be to discredit these books so that they are not believable. All that a person would have to do is insert a story about someone conjuring up dead spirits or possibly even insert a story of a Centaur (a mythological creature with the head, arms and torso of a human and the body and legs of a horse) and no one will believe any part of these books. Or, for that matter, all you have to do is change the meaning of just a couple of simple words and that will deceive practically everyone. For example, take the word "food" and change it to represent, "meat." Or take the word "month" and change it to represent, "moon."

I have not even begun to mention all of the things that the scribes have inserted into the Scriptures; things that should not have been put there. **Deuteronomy 4:2** says, "*you shall not add to the word which I command you, neither shall you diminish ought from it so that you may keep the commandments of the Sovereign your Creator which I command you.*"

By the time that you have finished reading this book you will have come to realize that the scribes have indeed corrupted and manipulated most, if not all, of the books of the Scriptures in one way or another.

Having said this, I truly believe that the Creator has preserved **His Truth** in the Scriptures for those of you who are truly searching for **"The Truth"**. To give you an example of what I am referring to, let's read the following verse. **John 18:4** says, "*Yeshua therefore, knowing all things that should come upon him, went forth and said unto them, whom do you seek"?*

So now then, can you think of a logical explanation as to why Yeshua (the Messiah) would know all the things that should come upon him? We can find the answer to this in **Luke 9:30-31,** which says, *"And, behold, there talked with him* (Yeshua) *two men, which were Moses and Elias: 31 Who appeared in majesty and spoke of his decease which he should accomplish at Yerusalem."*

Yeshua was not all knowing and all omniscient as we have been taught. These two verses of Scripture tell us that Moses and Elias spoke to Yeshua of his forthcoming demise, (death) and so that is how Yeshua would have known exactly what was going to happen to him when he went back to Yerusalem.

This is what I mean when I say that the Creator has preserved **The Truth** in the Scriptures even when the scribes and Pharisees have done every thing they can do to corrupt **The Truth** and lead us to the wrong conclusions.

3
Inherited Lies Versus The Traditions Of Men

Many times someone will want you to do something a particular way and when you ask them why they do it that particular way, they will tell you that this is how we have always done it and we are not going to change now. Most of the time this is ok, but it is not necessarily ok when it comes to things concerning the Scriptures.

Following the tradition of men or of the elders is frowned on in most Scripture verses. That is why the hair raises up on the back of my neck when I learn that we are doing something that is just a tradition which was passed down from one generation to another generation. **Mark 7:9** tells us, "*He* (the Messiah) *said unto them, you full well reject the commandment of the Sovereign, so that you may keep your own traditions.*"

I want to share a couple of short stories with you that may explain how easily we have all come to inherit some of our false beliefs and also show you how easily tradition can work its way into our everyday lives.

Cutting The Ends Off Of The Roast

One day the entire family went to great-grandma's home for a big meal. All of the women folk were in the kitchen cooking the fixings. They had a large roast to cook, and the youngest daughter was learning how to cook. The mother told her daughter that the first thing they needed to do was cut the ends off of the roast and put it into the pan.

When the young girl asked her mother why they had to cut the ends off of the roast, the mother told her daughter that this is what her mother had taught her to do.

So, the young girl went to her grandmother and asked her why they were supposed to cut the ends off of the roast before they put it into the pan. The grandmother told the girl that this is what her mother had taught her to do.

About that time the great-grandmother came in and overheard the last part of the conversation. Then they all turned to the great-grandmother and asked her why they were supposed to cut the ends off of the roast before they put it into the pan. She proceeded to tell them all that when she was a young girl all of the stoves were too small to put a large roasting pan in. She told them that now it was not necessary to cut off the ends of the roast since they now had larger stoves to cook their meals in.

This is just one example of how over-time, we have inherited a false tradition.

Let Me Count The Ways In Which We Have All Been Deceived

The Roman Chariots Of War & The US Space Shuttle

Can you think of how something which is as advanced and technical as the United States space shuttle and something as primitive as the historic Roman war chariots would be connected?

It turns out that the spacing of the chariots' wheels was exactly 4 feet, 8.5 inches apart. This was the spacing for the distance between the chariots wheels' axels because they had two large war horses pulling them. This in turn became the standard distance for the wheels on all wagons because they all had to follow in the ruts from the wagons in front of them.

When the people eventually traveled from Europe to America, they brought those same wagons over on the ships and the wheel spacing stayed the same width. Eventually when the rails were laid for the railroad tracks, they also stayed with the same width.

Today, the American space shuttle has two rocket boosters which are attached to the shuttle. These rocket boosters are manufactured in the state of Utah. Those same rocket boosters are shipped on railroad tracks that have to go through the tunnels which were carved out of the mountains for the trains back in the 1800's. Today, the rocket boosters cannot be manufactured any larger than they are because they would not be able to fit through those railroad tunnels.

This is how the US space industry, and the Roman chariots of war are connected. This is how the distance of 4 feet 8.5 inches which was used by the Romans was passed down through history and was eventually inherited by the US space industry.

Let Me Count The Ways In Which We Have All Been Deceived

As you can clearly see, it is easy to inherit ideas and traditions just from how you were raised or by the history that we have come from.

In the following pages, we will look at many more traditions that we have blindly accepted, as well as some of the ideas that we have ignorantly overlooked as we formed some of our established beliefs. It might surprise you to know just how many things you have been taught that are simply not true at all.

To give you an example of what I am referring to, answer this question: When were you taught that a new day begins? Many of you will say that we were taught that the new day begins at 12 o'clock midnight. How many times have you heard someone say, "Good Morning. It is midnight." Now if you will think about exactly what they said, you will realize that this statement is actually an oxymoron. Midnight has nothing whatsoever to do with morning. On the other hand, the Yahudian (Judean) and Messianic religious faiths have been taught that a new day begins at sunset when the sun goes down. This is simply something that they were taught. However, if we go to the Scripture, we will find that Scripture tells us something totally different. **Yeremiah 31:35** says, *"Thus saith the Sovereign, which gives <u>the sun for a light by day</u> and <u>the ordinances of the moon</u> and <u>the stars for a light by night</u>"...* According to this verse, **a new day begins when the sun comes up and it is night time when the stars come out.** Do you see how we have been wholeheartedly deceived about things that are in plain sight?

When I read in the Scriptures that the whole world would be deceived, I began to search in order to learn what specifically I had personally been deceived about.

As I have already stated, knowledge does not just make you smarter. Knowledge also makes you accountable.

Let Me Count The Ways In Which We Have All Been Deceived

Now is when I should warn you that if you continue to read any more of this book, you will be held personally accountable to a much higher standard. You will discover things that 99.9% of the world does not know or comprehend. Your preachers and your teachers cannot teach you these things because they were never taught these things either.

So now then, if you are prepared to have your entire belief system turned upside down, let's proceed.

Let Me Count The Ways In Which We Have All Been Deceived

4
What's In A Name?

The first thing that most of us do when we meet someone new is to shake hands and tell each other what our names are. This way, we will not be saying, "hey-you" all of the time. Names are very important. When you are in a crowd of people and someone yells out your name, you should be the only one who answers them. Names are passed down from generation to generation. When you sign your name to a contract, it is that signature that makes the contract binding.

Names can also become something that you can come to despise. If someone in your family has broken the law or has a bad reputation and someone asks you if you are related to that same individual, it might cause you to consider changing your name just so that you are not associated with that person or name any longer. There are a lot of people who have legally changed their names for that very reason.

In the next several pages, we are going to try to solve what some may call a puzzle or a riddle and possibly even a mystery about the true name of the Most High and his chosen people.

Genesis 10:21 tells us, *"Shem was the father of all of the children of Eber"...* According to **Wikipedia**, in

Yahudian (Jewish) folklore, Eber was the great-grandson of Shem. Eber was the only one who refused to help with the building of the Tower of Babel, so the Most High did not confuse his language when the tower was abandoned. Eber and his family alone retained the original human language; a language named after Eber, (Heber). So according to this understanding, the name, *"Eber"* is the root origin for the "(Hebrew) language." So now when we see the name, *"Eber"* we should automatically associate it with the Hebrew language. **Genesis 14:13** tells us, *"Abram was called a Hebrew."*

That being said, you need to understand that in the Scriptures the Hebrew names that a person has been given indicate the character of that individual. Notice, if you will that Abram's name was changed to Abraham. The name, *"Abram"* means, "Father", whereas, the name, *"Abraham"* means, "Father of many." You should also take note that once Abram's name was changed to Abraham, he was never called Abram ever again.

Genesis 17:1 says that *"when Abram was ninety years old and nine, the Creator appeared to Abram and said unto him, I am the Almighty Sovereign; walk before me and be thou <u>perfect</u>."*

Before we precede any further, we need to thoroughly understand what it means, in the Hebrew language, to be; "perfect."

There are several concordance books which break down the Hebrew and Greek words in your Scriptures into English. One of these books is called the **Strongest Strong's Concordance**. Another concordance book is the **Brown-Driver-Briggs Hebrew and English Lexicon**. These books use a standardized numerical system for every word that is used in the original Hebrew and Greek text. There is also a

Let Me Count The Ways In Which We Have All Been Deceived

computer program called **e-Sword** that does the very same thing.

I will be using the e-Sword program throughout this book to break down the meaning of the English words into the Hebrew and Greek definition. It is important to note that the letter that precedes the number indicates whether the word is a Hebrew word or a Greek word. The (H) represents a Hebrew word and the (G) represents a Greek word.

The following verse is an example of how e-Sword is represented on the computer program.

Genesis 17:1 says, "and when Abram[H87] was[H1961] ninety[H8673] years[H8141] old[H1121] and nine[H8672] Ehyeh[H1961] appeared[H7200] to[H413] Abram[H87] and said[H559] unto[H413] him, I[H589] am the Almighty[H7706] Sovereign[H410] walk[H1980] before[H6440] me and be[H1961] thou **perfect**."[H8549]

Perfect - H8549

תמים

tâmıym

taw-meem'

From H8552; *entire* (literally, figuratively, or morally); also (as noun) *integrity, truth:* - without blemish, complete, full, perfect, sincerely (-ity), sound, without spot, undefiled, upright (-ly), whole.

As you will see, the word "perfect" in both the **Strong's Concordance** and the **e-Sword** computer program has the same number, H8549:

The word **Perfect** is number **H8549**. It is written out in Hebrew as תמים. It is pronounced as **tâmîym**, *taw-meem'*. It is from H8552 meaning, *entire* (literally,

38

Let Me Count The Ways In Which We Have All Been Deceived

figuratively, or morally); also (as noun) *integrity, truth:* - without blemish, complete, full, perfect, sincerely (-ity), sound, without spot, undefiled, <u>upright</u> (-ly), whole.

You can see that I underlined the word **"upright."** The translators could have easily written this verse in the following way when they translated it from Hebrew to English. **Genesis 17:1,** *"... I am the Almighty Sovereign; walk before me and be thou <u>upright</u>."* Remember, we are trying to solve a mystery here. This word "upright" will soon become very important and significant.

Before Isaac was born to Abraham and Sarah, they both laughed when they heard that they would finally have a child in their old age. That is why they were told to name the child; "Isaac," which means, "laughter." So now you can see here that the name Isaac fit with the character of both his mother and father laughing.

When Isaac married Rebekah, she gave birth to twin boys. The first boy to arrive was Esau, who was considered the oldest. The second boy came out holding on to Esau's heel and so he was named Jacob (Yacob) which in Hebrew means, "To <u>deceive</u> or to supplant." Later on, when the two brothers grew up and became men, Yacob conned (deceived) Esau out of his birthright. And then, still later on Yacob tricked (deceived) his father Isaac into giving the family favoring to him instead of to his brother Esau. So, as you can see, Yacob lived up to the true character of his name; "deceiver" which was given to him when he was first born.

According to the **Book of Yubilees,** Yacob was 69 years old when his mother sent Yacob away to her brother Laban to flee from the wrath of his brother Esau's anger. Yacob lived with his uncle Laban in Mesopotamia for 20 years before he finally returned home to his mother and father with his 4 wives and 13 children. This would have

Let Me Count The Ways In Which We Have All Been Deceived

made Yacob at least a minimum of 89 or 90 years old when he returned home.

This is where the mystery concerning the name is beginning to thicken. In Scripture, there are two separate accounts concerning Yacob getting his name changed. We find these two separate accounts in **Genesis Chapter 32** and in **Genesis Chapter 35**.

The first account in **Chapter 32** tells us that Yacob camped at the Yabbok River, and he sent his servants and all of his livestock and his 4 wives with his 13 children on ahead of him to meet his brother Esau.

According to **Genesis 32:24-28**, *"Yacob was left alone; and a man wrestled with him there until the breaking of the day."* Notice if you will, that this says that Yacob wrestled with a man. Yacob did not wrestle with an angel (Malakim) as we have all been taught. Yacob wrestled with a man. It goes on to say that they wrestled all night until daybreak and when neither one could win the man dislocated a joint in Yacob's thigh. Now if you have ever had this happen to you, you will know that it is very painful. You can hardly stand, let alone, walk upright. But Yacob was able to stand up and walk upright. Before the two men parted ways, the man favored Yacob and called him by a new name.

As I said before, names in Hebrew represent a person's character. Yacob was walking upright. According to e-Sword the Hebrew word for upright is **"Yasher."** It is number H3477.

Upright - H3477

ישר

yâshâr
yaw-shawr'

From H3474; *straight* (literally or figuratively): - convenient, equity, Jasher, just, meet (-est), + pleased well right (-eous), straight, (most) upright (-ly, -ness).

The plural word for Yasher is "*Yeshurun.*" The root word for Yasher is "*Asher.*" This name "Asher" will become very important shortly. Deductive reasoning causes us to conclude that the man called Yacob, "Yasher."

Ok, by now you are thinking to yourself, that is not what it says. It says that the man changed Yacob's name to, "Israel." Is that not what you were thinking? Well this is exactly what the scribes want you to believe. **Exodus 23:13** tells us that we are to, *"make no mention of the name of other gods, neither let it be heard out of your mouth."*

Question? Do you have any idea of where the etymology of the name, "Israel" is from? Is it just a coincidence that the name, Israel or "Is-Ra-El" incorporates the names of three pagan gods / goddesses?

1. The first name is, "*Isis.*" Isis was an Egyptian throne goddess dating back to the 5th dynasty. Her name literally means the feminine aspect of the throne–also the queen of the throne (heaven).

2. The second name is "*Ra.*" Ra was the name of the sun god of Heliopolis in ancient Egypt.

3. The third name is "*El.*" El was the name of a god of the Canaanite, or Levantine religion as a whole. El was also known as the father of humanity and all creatures and he was the husband of the goddess Asherah (groves) as recorded in the clay tablets of Ugarit. The image of the bull

Let Me Count The Ways In Which We Have All Been Deceived

was symbolic to El and his son Baal. (We will discover who Baal is shortly.)

Can you tell me what the 1st **Commandment** says? **Exodus 20:3** says, *"You shall have no other gods before me."* Are you beginning to understand that Yacob did not have his name changed to the triple pagan name of *"IS-RA-EL"* as the Scriptures tell us that it was?

Before we get ahead of ourselves, let's look at those other additional verses that tell us of Yacob getting his name changed to "Is-ra-el." We find these just three chapters later in **Genesis, Chapter 35**. We find in **verse 7** of this chapter that Yacob went from Shechem to Bethel. It was here that Yacob built an altar, and he called the place *"Elbethel."* **Verse 10** is where it says that it was the Most High, instead of a man whom he had wrestled with, who changed Yacob's name to Israel. **Genesis 35:10** says, *"And the Sovereign said unto him, your name is Yacob: your name shall not be called any more Yacob, but Israel shall be your name: and he called his name Israel."*

Once again, do you see a problem here with this name of *"Elbethel"*? The name, *"Bethel"* means, "house of god." So here is a question: Which deity does this house actually belong to? It tells us right here that this was the pagan deity; "El's" house. We just learned that "El" was a deity of the Canaanite people.

You may recall that it was in Bethel that Yeroboam established a place of false worship when he set up the statue of a **bull** for the people to worship so that they would not need to return to Yerusalem to worship. **1 Kings 12:28-29** says, **28** *"Whereupon Yeroboam took counsel and made two calves* (Bulls) *of gold and said unto them, it is too much for you to go up to Yerusalem: behold your gods, O Yeshurun, which brought you up out of the land of Egypt.* **29** *And he set the one in Bethel and he put the other in*

42

Dan." You can clearly see by now, that this is a completely different story than the first one in **Chapter 32**. Do you remember what I told you back on page 24? I said that if you have two different versions in Scripture, then one of them has to be erroneous?

So then, what exactly did the scribes do here? We have pretty well concluded that the second version of the story was more than likely inaccurate. But now what about the first story in **Genesis Chapter 32**? Do you remember that when the Most High changed Abram's name to Abraham, he was never called Abram again? If you will pay close attention, you will see that even after both of these two stories in **Genesis**, Yacob is still called Yacob. The first story is more accurate because the man did not actually change Yacob's name. What he did was call Yacob by his physical character which was, "<u>upright</u>." The man saw that Yacob was standing and walking Yasher (upright) so that is what he called him. Yacob would not have accepted the name of Israel. The name, "Is-ra-el", would have been an insult to Yacob. So, from now on, when you see in the Scriptures that it says, "**the children of Israel**", you need to mentally insert the name, "Yasher." This way it will be, "**the children of Yasher**" or "**the children of the Upright.**" You need to completely delete the name of Israel from your vocabulary.

Later on, in **Exodus Chapter 3** we find the story of Moses and the burning bush. **Exodus 3:6** says, "*Moreover He said, I am the Sovereign of your father, the Sovereign of Abraham, the Sovereign of Isaac and <u>the Sovereign of Yacob</u>.*" Did you notice that He <u>did not say</u> that He was the Sovereign of Israel?

You might recall that Moses grew up in the Pharaoh's palace in Egypt. He also went to school with Pharaoh's son. So, Moses would have known all about all of the false pagan gods that the Egyptians worshiped. He

Let Me Count The Ways In Which We Have All Been Deceived

would have learned what each of the pagan gods' names were.

When Moses was 80 years old, he was out taking care of his father-in-law's herds when he saw a burning bush up on the mountain of Horeb and so he went to check it out. When Moses got close enough, he heard a voice speak to him from heaven. The voice told Moses to take off his shoes because he was walking on set-apart ground.

As the story goes, Ehyeh tells Moses that He has seen the affliction of His people who are in Egypt, and He has come down (from heaven) to deliver His people. **Exodus 3:10** says, *"Come now therefore and I will send you unto Pharaoh, so that you may bring forth my people, the children of Yeshurun* (the upright) *out of Egypt."*

This is where this entire subject about the name is beginning to get interesting. You will remember that I told you that the first thing that most of us do when we meet someone new is to tell them who we are. Well right here is where Moses specifically asks the Most High Creator what His name is. **Exodus 3:13-15** says, 13 *"and Moses said unto the Sovereign, behold, when I come unto the children of Yeshurun and shall say unto them, the Sovereign of your fathers has sent me unto you; and they shall say to me, What is His name? What shall I say unto them?* 14 *And the Sovereign said unto Moses,* ***I AM THAT I AM****: and He said, Thus shall you say to the children of Yeshurun,* ***I AM*** *has sent me unto you.* 15 *And the Sovereign said moreover unto Moses, thus shall you say unto the children of Yeshurun, the* **LORD***, Sovereign of your fathers, the Sovereign of Abraham, the Sovereign of Isaac and the Sovereign of Yacob, has sent me unto you: this is my name forever and this is my memorial to all generations."*

The following excerpt is taken from page 117 of the JPS Hebrew – English Tanakh. The (JPS) represents the

Let Me Count The Ways In Which We Have All Been Deceived

Jewish Publication Society. This is the only English version of Scripture that I have found which has the Fathers name written out as it actually should be written. It is **<u>Ehyeh – Asher – Ehyeh</u>**.

What is interesting is that this is the only time that it is written like this in this book.

> ¹³Moses said to God, "When I come to the Israelites and say to them, 'The God of your fathers has sent me to you,' and they ask me, 'What is His name?' what shall I say to them?" ¹⁴And God said to Moses, "Ehyeh-Asher-Ehyeh."ᵃ He continued, "Thus shall you say to the Israelites, 'Ehyehᵇ sent me to you.'" ¹⁵And God said further to Moses, "Thus shall you speak to the Israelites: The LORD,ᶜ the God of your fathers, the God of Abraham, the God of Isaac, and the God of Jacob, has sent me to you:
> This shall be My name forever,

This is from **Exodus 3:13-15.**

Whoa, stop the presses! Did you just see what the scribes have done in these two previous verses? Any time you see <u>any</u> words written in all capital letters you need to sit up and take notice. This is a good indication that the scribes have done something to this. As a matter of fact, the scribes have actually succeeded in orchestrating a <u>triple deception</u> in the previous paragraph. This is very confusing and may be hard to completely understand, but I will do my best to make sense of it.

As you can clearly see, the words; *"I AM THAT I AM"* and the word *"LORD"* are all in capital letters. Do you remember what I said about Shem being the father of all of the children of Eber? The name, *"Eber"* is synonymous with

45

Let Me Count The Ways In Which We Have All Been Deceived

the word "*Hebrew*." Let's take a look at those same words in the Hebrew language.

According to e-Sword the words "**I AM**" is number H1961.

I AM - H1961

היה

hâyâh

haw-yaw'

A primitive root (compare H1933); to *exist*, that is, *be* or *become, come to pass.*

This is how it is written out in English: **Ahayeh or Eyah or Ehyeh**.

The word "**THAT**" is number H834.
That - H834

אֲשֶׁר

'ăsher

ash-er'

A primitive relative pronoun (of every gender and number); *who, which, what, that;* also (as adverb and conjunction) *when, where, how, because, in order that,* etc:

Once again, before we precede any further, I need to explain something else to you. You know how there are several words in the English language that have more than one meaning. Well, we have the same issue here with the Hebrew word "Asher."

This word "**Asher**" also has a completely different meaning with a different numerical value assigned to it. That number is H833.

Asher - H833

אשר

'âshar

aw-shar

A primitive root; to *be straight* (used in the widest sense, especially to *be level, right, happy*); figuratively to *go forward, be honest, prosper* or in other words, to be of an upright character.

What the scribes have done in this case was to switch the meaning of the word "Asher." The *I AM THAT I AM* is written out in Hebrew like this; **"אהיה אהי אשר."** It should now be pronounced as **"Ehyeh Asher Ehyeh."** The scribes using the definition to the word "that" instead of the word "Asher" was the second deception.

Ok, now let's look at the third deception that the scribes have thrust upon us unsuspecting readers. I am referring to the word **"LORD."** As I said before, it is in capital letters, which makes us take notice that the scribes have tampered with this word as well. Do you know what the etymology of the word **"LORD"** is from?

We find that it says in the **Brown-Driver-Briggs Hebrew** and the **English Lexicon Concordance** that the name, **"LORD"** is associated with the Canaanite and Philistine god named **"Baal."**

So now since the scribes have inserted the name, **"LORD"** in the place of **"Baal"**, don't you believe that it would be a good idea for us to also take the name of **"LORD"** out of our vocabulary as well? As a matter of fact, Scripture tells us that very thing. **Hosea 2:16-17** says, "*It* *shall be at that day, saith Ehyeh that you shall call me Ishi* (husband); *and shall no longer call me <u>Baali</u>,* (**the LORD**). *For I will take away the names of <u>Baalim</u> out of her mouth and they shall no more be remembered by their name."*

Well now, are you just about ready to solve this mystery - puzzle - riddle concerning the vital importance of the name? Several verses in Scripture allude to the fact that the name is very important. **Proverbs 22:1** says, "<u>A good name</u> *is to be chosen rather than great wealth*"... **Ecclesiastes 7:1** says, "<u>A good name</u> *is better than precious ointment*"... **Song of Solomon 1:3** *says,* "*Because of the savor of thy good ointments thy <u>name</u> is as ointment poured forth, therefore do the virgins love thee."* And **Yeremiah 33:9** says, "*... it shall be to me <u>a name of joy, praise and honor</u>*"...

We have now concluded that the true correct name of the Creator is "**Ehyeh <u>Asher</u> Ehyeh**." We also found out that Shem was the father of all Eber. Can you, by chance, tell me what the name, "Shem" actually means in the Hebrew language? According to e-Sword the name, "**Shem**" is number <u>H8035</u>.

<u>Shem - H8035</u>

שֵׁם

shêm

The same as <u>H8034</u>; *name*; *Shem*, a son of Noah (often including his posterity): - Sem, Shem.

Shem actually means "<u>name</u>".

Abraham was told to walk "<u>Yasher</u>" (upright). We have also determined by deductive reasoning that the name that the man who wrestled with Yacob actually called him, "Yasher." We have also concluded that the plural term for "Yasher" is "**Yeshurun**."

Now I have a question for you. Did you know that the name, "Yeshurun" is mentioned four separate times in the Scriptures? **Deuteronomy 32:15** says, *"But **Yeshurun** waxed fat and kicked ...* **Deuteronomy 33:5** says, *"And he was king in **Yeshurun** ...* **Deuteronomy 33:26** says, *"There is none like unto the Sovereign of **Yeshurun** ...* And finally, **Isaiah 44:2** says, *"Thus saith Ehyeh that made you and formed you from the womb, which will help you; fear not, O Yacob, my servant; thou, **Yesurun**, whom I have chosen."*

Periodically we will see a sign along the side of the road that someone has put up which reads as follows: **2 Chronicles 7:14** says, *"If my people, which are called by my name, shall humble themselves and pray and seek my face and turn from their wicked ways; then will I hear from heaven and will forgive their sin and will heal their land."*

This verse sums up this entire subject matter of the importance of who the chosen people of the Most High are. They have to be called by the name of **Asher** which is the root word for "Yasher", which means they are the **children of Yeshurun**. These people will have the character of the **Upright**.

There is a reason why I started off with the topic of the name. You may have noticed that I do not use the titles of God or LORD. This is because I have discovered that the name of the Creator is "**Ehyeh Asher Ehyeh.**" **The Third (3rd) Commandment** tells us in **Exodus 20:7** that, *"you shall not take the name of Ehyeh your Sovereign in vain; for Ehyeh will not hold him guiltless that takes His name in vain."* **Ezekiel 39:7** says, *"I will make my set-apart name known in the midst of my people Yeshurun; and I will not let them pollute my set-apart name anymore: and the* *heathen shall know that I am Ehyeh, the set-apart One among the Upright."*

One of the biggest deceptions that the scribes have perpetuated on the masses can be found in **Genesis 4:26**. It says, *"and to Seth, to him also there was born a son; and he called his name Enos: then <u>began</u> men to call upon the name of Ehyeh."* On the surface, this verse seems to be a simple statement. However, when you check to see what the word "**began**" means in the Hebrew language you will see that it does not mean what you might think it means. According to e-Sword the word "**began**" is number <u>H2490</u>.

<u>began - H2490</u>

חלל

châlal

khaw-lal'

A primitive root (compare <u>H2470</u>); properly to *bore*, that is, (by implication) to *wound*, to *dissolve*; figuratively **<u>to profane</u>** (a person, place, or thing), to *break* (one's word), etc.

This is telling us that it was at the time when Enos was born that mankind started defiling the name of Ehyeh. They were effectively making it worthless. Today the Yahudians tell us that the name of the Creator is so kodesh, (set-apart / special) that they believe that they are not to even let it come out of their mouths. This is why when they speak the name of the Creator, they call Him "Hashem." Do you know why they use the name Hashem? The word "Hashem" in Hebrew actually means; "The name." By saying the name, "Hashem", they are in all reality guilty of breaking the **4th Commandment**. They are in fact making the Creator's name vain or worthless.

Let Me Count The Ways In Which We Have All Been Deceived

By now you may be thinking to yourself, how can this be? Why would mankind stop speaking the true name of Ehyeh? Well, it turns out that we can also get that answer from the Scriptures. **Yeremiah 44:26** says, *"Therefore hear you the word of Ehyeh, all Yahuda that dwell in the land of Egypt; Behold, I have sworn by <u>my great name</u>, saith Ehyeh that <u>my name shall no longer be spoken in the mouth of any man of Yahuda</u> in all of the land of Egypt, saying, Ehyeh the Sovereign lives."*

(Note): **When you get an opportunity, read the entire Chapter of Yeremiah 44 and you will see exactly what the Yahudians were doing, which caused Ehyeh to take His name out of the mouths of the Yahudians.**

Take note if you will, of the following verses in **Isaiah**, speaking about the importance of the name.

1. **Isaiah 29:23** says, *"But when he sees his children, the work of my hands, in the midst of him, <u>they shall set-apart my name</u> and set-apart the set-apart One of Yacob and shall fear the Sovereign of the Upright."*

2. **Isaiah 43:7** says, *"Even <u>everyone that is called by my name</u>: for I have created him for my majesty, I have formed him; yes, I have made him."*

3. **Isaiah 47:4** says, *"As for our redeemer, <u>Ehyeh of hosts is his name</u>, the set-apart One of the Upright."*

Did you know that the name of Ehyeh is in the New Testament? And did you also know that there is power in the name of Ehyeh? To see this, we turn to **John Chapter 18**. This is where Yudas (Judas) came with an entire army garrison of 300 to 700 men with officers and chief priests and Pharisees who had all brought weapons and torches with them to arrest Yeshua in the garden. **Verse 4** is where it starts to become interesting. **John 18:4-6** says, 4 *"Yeshua therefore, knowing all things that should come upon him, went forth and said unto them, whom do you seek? 5 They answered him, Yeshua of Nazareth. Yeshua saith unto them, I am he. And Yudas also, which betrayed him, stood with them. 6 As soon then as he had said unto them, I am he, they went backward and fell to the ground."*

Do you see it here in **verses 5 and 6**? If you will look in your **King James Version of the Scriptures**, you can see that the *"he"* that following after the "I am" is in italics. This means that the scribes have inserted the word "he" in there to throw us off. Yeshua did not say; "I am *he.*" What Yeshua actually did was to audibly pronounce the name of the Father. Yeshua said; **"Ehyeh."** **Verse 6** shows us the true power of the name. It says, *"As soon then as he had said unto them;* **"Ehyeh"***, they went backward and fell to the ground."*

Now just imagine for a moment, what it must have looked like when that entire army garrison of men were getting up off the ground, looking at each other and saying to one another, "What the heck just happened?"

Let's look at another time when the scribes have tried to hide the name of Ehyeh when Yeshua was proclaiming His name. **John 14:6** says, *"Yeshua said unto him;* **"Ehyeh"** *is the way, The Truth and the life: no man cometh unto the Father, but by me."*

We also find that the scribes have hidden Ehyeh's name in plain sight four separate times in the Book of Revelation.

1. **Revelation 1:8** says, *"I am* (Ehyeh) *is the Aleph and the Tov, the beginning and the ending, saith Ehyeh, which is, and which was, and which is to come."*

52

2. **Revelation 1:11** says, "*I am* (Ehyeh) *is the Aleph and the Tov, the first and the last*"....

3. **Revelation 21:6** says, "*...It is done. I am* (Ehyeh) *is the Aleph and the Tov, the beginning and the end.*"

4. And finally, **Revelation 22:13** says, "*I am* (Ehyeh) *is the Aleph and the Tov, the beginning and the end, the first and the last.*"

(Note): The Alpha and the Omega are Greek words. They should have been using the Hebrew words here, which is the Aleph and the Tav. The Aleph is the first letter in the Hebrew alphabet and the Tav is the last letter in the Hebrew alphabet.

We find in **Ezekiel Chapter 9** that "*six men* (Malakim) *are called who have charge over the city and have destroying weapons with them. One was clothed in linen, and he had a writer's inkhorn by his side.*" **Ezekiel 9:4** says, "*that Ehyeh called to the man and Ehyeh said unto him, go through the midst of the city, through the midst of Yerusalem and <u>set a mark upon the foreheads of the men</u> who sigh and cry for all of the abominations that are done in the midst thereof.*" It goes on to say that the other five men (Malakim) are told to go and kill every man, woman, and child–young or old–who does not have the mark upon their forehead.

Can you think of what this mark might possibly be that the man put on their foreheads? **Revelation 7:3-4** says, "*hurt not the earth, neither the sea, nor the trees, <u>until we have sealed the servants of our Sovereign in their foreheads. And I heard the number of them which were sealed:</u>* **4** <u>*and there were sealed a hundred and forty and four thousand from all of the tribes of the children of Yeshurun.*</u>" These are the 144,000 elect who are chosen to make up the members of the New Yerusalem which will come down from heaven. But this still does not tell us what the mark is that was placed in their foreheads does it? We find that answer in the following two verses of Scripture. **Revelation 14:1** says, *"...a hundred forty and four thousand, having his Father's name written in their foreheads"* and **Revelation 22:4** *says, "And they shall see his face; and his name shall be in their foreheads."*

Henceforth, when I am writing out the name of the Most High Creator, I will be writing it out as; "**Ehyeh.**" This way I will not be violating the 3rd **Commandment**, found in **Exodus 20:7** which says, *"You shall not take the name of Ehyeh your Sovereign in vain; for Ehyeh will not hold him guiltless that takes His name in vain."* **Exodus 3:15** *tells us that the name of Ehyeh is forever.* It says *this is my memorial to all generations."*

I will end this discussion about the name of the Creator with the story about the ten virgins in **Matthew Chapter 25**. Five of the virgins were wise and five of them were unwise. Five of them did not have enough oil to keep their lamps lit, so they had to go buy more oil. While they were gone, the Messiah came and closed the door to the wedding banquet. The five virgins who did not have enough oil showed up and wanted in. The Messiah told them to go away because, he said, *"I know you not."* Now here is the question that people have been asking for a long, long time. What does the oil represent? We can go to Scripture and discover the answer to that question. **Song of Solomon 1:3** says that it is, *"Because of the savor of your good ointments your name is as ointment poured forth, therefore do the virgins love you."* According to this riddle, the oil that the five wise virgins had actually represented the name of Ehyeh. They knew his name and they used his name. It was because they had the oil, (the name), that they were permitted into the wedding banquet.

Let Me Count The Ways In Which We Have All Been Deceived

There are approximately 500 verses in Scripture which either allude to or directly mention the importance of Ehyeh's <u>name</u>. They are as follows:

- My name: 117 times.
- Great name: 6 times.
- His name: 104 times.
- Name of Ehyeh: 103 times.
- Thy name: 118 times.
- Set-apart name: 21 times.
- By name: 6 times.

It is of paramount importance that we know the true name of our Creator. It is even more important that we actually use Ehyeh's name. Yeshua declared the Father's name. So should we.

It is just as important that we have the Upright Character of the Father, so that we can be accounted as the children of Yeshurun and have the name of Asher in our character and our foreheads (minds).

5
Interpretation

I first like to ask people what kind of car they drive. Then I ask them if they had a Ford, would they use a Chevy or Dodge manual when they work on their Ford. They automatically say, "Of course not." This is because the definitions and specification are more than likely different on the different kinds of automobiles.

I say that because when we read the Scriptures today, we need to remember that the times and the cultures were different back when the Scriptures were written. We cannot always take something that was written way back then and apply it to our present time in the same manner.

Several years ago, I read a short, one-page article about how Constantine was able to round up many of the Sabbath keeping Yahudians. The article said that spies were paid to watch the homes in the area during the winter time. When the spies saw a home that did not have smoke coming up out of the chimney on the Sabbaths, they had a good idea that these people were Sabbath keeping Yahudians. This is because these people were following the instructions telling them not to be *"kindling a fire on the Sabbath day."* **Exodus 35:3** says, *"You shall kindle no fire throughout your habitations upon the Sabbath day."*

Let Me Count The Ways In Which We Have All Been Deceived

This verse, by itself, appears to be pretty cut and dry. But did Ehyeh really want the people to do without heat on the Sabbath day during the cold winter days? Do you believe that is really what Ehyeh's intent was when He spoke that command? Am I out of line when I say that we need to consider what was said in the verse prior to this? **Exodus 35:2** says, *"Six days shall work be done, but on the seventh day there shall be to you a set-apart day, a Sabbath of rest to Ehyeh: Whosoever does work therein shall be put to death."*

We need to look at the content of what was being said. Let's read it again in context. **Exodus 35:2-3** says, 2 *"...Whosoever does work therein shall be put to death. 3 You shall kindle no fire throughout your habitations upon the Sabbath day."* Could this possibly be saying that you shall not be lighting a fire and working with the fire on the Sabbath day?

The word "kindle" is used several times in Scripture. The word "kindle" is used at least two separate times to imply anger or wrath. Could it in all probability be saying that you shall not start an argument or provoke someone to anger on the Sabbath day? I believe that this is what it really means when it says you shall not kindle a fire on the Sabbath day.

I have a friend who will not drive an automobile on the Sabbath day because he realized that the sparkplugs create a fire when the car is running.

I personally have a hard time believing that Ehyeh would want everyone to freeze in their cold homes on the Sabbath days during the cold winter months. There are some places that are cold enough that a heat stove is needed as much as seven or eight months out of the year. The grown men and women who are living in these homes may be able to handle the cold. But what about the young children and babies who are in the houses? Is this really the correct interpretation for the meaning of not kindling a fire, or could it possibly be something as simple as not starting an argument?

Can you imagine how many people have strictly obeyed this command and have suffered through all of those cold Sabbaths for years because they refused to light a fire and heat their homes? What if they have done this their entire lives and it turned out that this was not what it really meant when it said, *"Thou shall not kindle a fire on the Sabbath day"*?

Please do not misunderstand what I am saying. I am not saying that the people are wrong to do this. I am just trying to show you that there are many things in Scripture that are not necessarily as simple to interpret as they first seem to be.

Let Me Count The Ways In Which We Have All Been Deceived

6
Where Did The Letter "J" Come From?

I have already mentioned the **1611 Edition of the King James Version of Scripture** once before, but I want to bring it up once again. This version of Scripture is somewhat hard to read because it does not use certain particular letters in the same way that we see them used today.

The first thing that you will realize when you begin reading this book is that, in many places, the "u" is used in the place of the "v." Words such as *heaven, moved, divided* and *evening*, for example, are written as *heauen, mooued, diuided* and *euening*.

The publishers of this book also used the letter "v" in the place of the "u" in words such as "*vpon*" instead of "*upon*" and "*vp*" instead of "*up*."

The letter "f" is also used many times in the place of the "s." A couple of examples of this are in the words *first, instituted, promised, incest* and *servant*. These words are written out with an "f" instead of an "s" in this manner: *firft, inftituted, promifed, inceft* and *feruant*.

Let Me Count The Ways In Which We Have All Been Deceived

You will also find that the "I" and the "y" are swapped in many of the words. Words such as "dry" and "fly" and "genealogy" are spelled out with an "ie" instead of with a "y" like this; *drie, flie* and *genealogie.*

I have made a point of showing you all of this so that you can see that this was how the Scriptures were written back prior to the 1600s. This is simply how the people wrote back in those days.

I have a particularly special reason for showing you all of this. There is one letter that is not used at all in this 1611 version of the Scriptures. That letter is the "J." Did you know that prior to the 1600s there was not even a "J" in the English alphabet?

I am pretty sure you noticed in the previous chapters that there were words that started with a "J" such as "Jasher" and "Jeshurun" and "Jacob" that I have changed to begin with a "Y." When I wrote these words out, I usually used the "Y." For instance, there was Yasher and Yeshurun and Yacob.

Technically speaking, there should not be any names used in the Scriptures that have a "J" in them. Names such as Jacob, Jerusalem, Yeremiah, Jews, Judas and Joseph should be spelled as Yacob, Yerusalem, Yeremiah, Yahuda, Yudas and Yoseph.

The question that I want you to ask yourself is; where did the name of "Jesus" come from in our modern-day versions of Scripture? Of all of the letters in the alphabet, the scribes have started the name of the deliverer with a letter that did not even exist prior to the 1600's. Does that not sound highly suspicious?

As you have probably noticed in the previous pages of this book, I do not call the Deliverer by the false name that the scribes and the Pharisees have given to him. I

60

personally call him "Yeshua" which is more in line with the actual Hebrew name of "Isaiah or Yeshua." In all reality, the name of "Isaiah" should also be pronounced as "Yeshua."

There is not any specific source to refer you to in order to learn where the name, "Jesus" originated from. However, one source that I found says, **"The name "Jesus" is from the Greek name Iesus, which is derived from a Greek goddess. It's also connected to the Greek god Zeus. In the Spanish language the name Jesus is pronounced (Hey-Zeus)."** Now isn't that very interesting?

The **1611 Version of Scripture** was published a little over 400 years ago and no one was calling the deliverer by the name of "Jesus" back then. Today, the false scribes and Pharisees are telling everyone that there is only one name under heaven by which mankind can be saved and that name is "Jesus."

Since you have already read the previous chapter, you now know that "Ehyeh" is the only name that will save mankind. It is not "Jesus." **Isaiah 47:4** says, *"As for our redeemer, Ehyeh of hosts is his name, the set-apart One of Yeshurun."*

7
Speaking The Names Of False Deity

I have discovered two separate sources that say there are between 6800 and 6900 distinct languages in the modern world today. The Mandarin Chinese language is spoken by approximately 14.5% of the people in the world. I was completely surprised to find that, according to **Wikipedia**, less than 6 percent of the world population speaks the English language. However, I was not surprised to find that the Hebrew language is spoken by less than .01% of the world population.

It was at the Tower of Babel that Ehyeh caused the people to change their languages. This is where we get the word "babble" from. **Revelation Chapter 18** is speaking about Babylon. **Revelation 18:4** says, "*I heard another voice from heaven, saying, <u>Come out of her,</u> (Babylon) <u>my people,</u> so that you be not partakers of her sins and that you receive not of her plagues.*"

The terms "Babylon" and "babble" are synonymous with miscommunication and confusion. This is why we have upwards of 33000 separate Protestant denominations in the world today. Each denomination has its own

Let Me Count The Ways In Which We Have All Been Deceived

distinctive beliefs that distinguish them from everyone else. Some are strict, while others are liberal. Some are very strict, while others are very liberal.

As I have already stated back in chapter four, Scripture tells us that we are not to even speak the names of any other false deity. **Exodus 23:13** actually says, "<u>to make no mention of the name of other mighty ones, neither let it be heard out of your mouth.</u>" **Yoshua 23:7** also says, "<u>... neither make mention of the name of their mighty ones, nor cause to swear by them, neither serve them, nor bow yourselves to them.</u>"

So then take a moment, if you will and think about all of the names of all of the false gods that you speak of on a daily basis. Can you think of any that you know of? **Proverbs 18:21** tells us, "*Life and death are in the power of the tongue:*

Proverbs 4:24 says to, "*Turn away from you a crooked mouth and put perverse lips far from you.*" This is not necessarily speaking of cleaning up our foul mouths. This goes far beyond cuss words and filthy jokes that some of us are prone to blurt out of our mouths.

Zephaniah 3:9 says, "*I will return to the people <u>a pure language</u>, so that they may all <u>call upon the name of Ehyeh</u>, to serve him <u>with one consent</u>.*" There is only one way to serve Ehyeh, not hundreds or thousands of ways. **Zephaniah 3:13** goes on to say that "*the remnant of Yeshurun shall not do iniquity, nor speak lies; neither shall a deceitful tongue be found in their mouth*":

Would it surprise you to know that all of the English names of the week are derived from the names of false pagan deities? A lot of heathen nations worship the sun. This is where we get the name of "<u>Sun-day.</u>" According to the Scriptures, the 1st day of the week is called; "day number one."

Let Me Count The Ways In Which We Have All Been Deceived

Other heathen nations worshiped the moon. This is where we get the name of "Mon-day." According to the Scriptures, the 2nd day of the week is called; "day number two."

The name of "Tues-day" comes from the Norse deity named Tyr. He was the deity of war. He was a son of Odin. According to the Scriptures, the 3rd day of the week is called; "day number three."

The name of "Wednes-day" originated from the name of Odin or Wodin, who was considered the most powerful deity in Norse mythology. According to the Scriptures, the 4th day of the week is called; "day number four."

The name of "Thurs-day" came from another Norse deity, Thor. According to Norse mythology, Thor was also the son of Odin. According to the Scriptures, the 5th day of the week is called; "day number five."

The name of "Fri-day" originated from the name of the Norse goddess named Frigg. She was the wife of Odin. According to the Scriptures, the 6th day of the week is called; "day number six."

The name of "Satur-day" originates from worship of the planet Saturn. According to the Scriptures, the 7th day of the week is called; the "Sabbath" day. This is the only day of the week that Ehyeh set-apart as the day of rest.

Are you beginning to see how we have ignorantly inherited these pagan names into our vocabulary and not one preacher has ever told you that it is wrong to even speak these names?

Now let's look at the names of the months of the year. Would it surprise you to find that many of them are in fact named after false mighty ones also?

The calendar that we use today was in actuality inherited from the Roman Empire. It is actually called the

Let Me Count The Ways I Was Deceived

Gregorian calendar... because it was named for and authorized by Pope Gregory XIII in 1582. The original Roman calendar began in the month of March, which is natural since this is when the flowers spring and the renewal of agricultural activity began. It originally only had ten named months in the year. In about 700 B.C. Numa Pompilius, the second king of Rome, attempted to regularize the Roman calendar by defining the two bleak winter months. He called them January and February. The Romans spoke Latin and so the last 4 months of the year lined up with Latin numerology: September for "sept", which is (7), October for "oct", which is (8), November for "nov", which is (9) and December for "dec", which is (10).

The name for the month of "January" was named after the deity named "Janus." His festival was held in this month. Janus was the deity of gates and doorways, beginnings, and endings. So, it seemed to be an appropriate month to begin the New Year.

The name for the month of "February" originated from the Latin word "Februa." It is for the false festival of purification.

The name for the month of "March" originated from the planet "Mars". He was the Roman deity of War. March was the original beginning of the year and the time for the continuation of war.

The name of the month of "April" comes from the Greek goddess named "Aphrodite." She is the Greek goddess of love and beauty.

The name of the month of "May" comes from the Latin name "Maia." She was the Italic goddess of spring.

The name of the month of "June" comes from the Latin name of "Juno." She was the principal goddess of the Roman Pantheon. She was the goddess of marriage. There are more marriages performed in the month of June than any other month of the year.

The name for the month of "<u>July</u>" originated from "Julius" Caesar himself in 46 BC. The people worshiped the Caesars as if they were gods themselves. Julius Caesar reformed the Roman calendar and in the process, he named this month after himself.

The name for the month of "<u>August</u>" originated from "Augustus" Caesar himself, as well. As I said before, the people worshiped the Caesars as if they were gods. Augustus Caesar clarified and completed the calendar reform of Julius Caesar. In the process, he also named this month after himself.

As you can clearly see, the name of at least 7 of the 12 names of the months originated from the names of false pagan deities.

Did you know that the months of the year do actually have names assigned to them by Ehyeh himself? We will get into that later on in the next chapter.

As I said earlier, we have been taught to speak the names of all of these false mighty ones and not a one of your preachers or teachers have told you that this is wrong, because they have been deceived just like you have been. If you think that this is bad, hold on to your seat, because I intend to show you that this is not the half of it.

Did you know that practically every word that you have been taught to use in praise and worship actually originated from the names of false mighty ones?

As I have already mentioned before, I use the word "<u>Scriptures</u>" instead of the word "Bible." I do it for two reasons. The first reason I do not use the word is that I use additional books other than the 66 books that are in the modern-day versions to read from. The second reason I do not use the word "Bible" is that this word originated from the city of Byblis.

The papyrus or paper, which all documents were originally written on, was imported from Egypt through the Phoenician seaport of Gebal, which the Greeks called Byblos or Byblus. This city was the home of a Phoenician Sun-deity. The sun-deity was associated with the "Lady of Biblos." Both the city of Byblos in Phoenicia and the city Byblis in Egypt were named after the female deity Byblis (also called Byble or Biblis). This deity was supposedly the grand-daughter of Apollo, the Greek sun-deity. Byblia was also a name for Venus, a goddess of sensuality among the ancient Greeks. - The proper term to use instead of the name of the Bible is the "**Scriptures**."

As you may have noticed, I use the words "set-apart" instead of the word "Holy." This is because the word "Holy" comes from the name of "Holi", which is the great Hindu spring festival that was held in honor of Krishna, the spring sun deity. The word for set-apart in Hebrew is actually "Kodesh." The proper words to use in order to avoid speaking the name of a false mighty one is, "**set-apart**."

Let's look at another word which we use all of the time when we sing. The word "Glory" comes from the Latin word "Gloria" which is identified with the sun as being radiant, shining, brilliant, bright as the sun. "Gloria" was a Roman goddess who was half-naked, and she held the zodiac signs. The proper word to use is, "**esteem**" or "**majesty**."

The word "church" comes from the Anglo-Saxon root word "circe." It stems from the name of the Greek goddess "Circe", the daughter of "Helios." The proper word to use is, "**assembly**." It is referring to the people themselves who are attending the service, not the building itself.

The "Cross" was originally used as a symbol of the mystical "Tau" the Babylonian - Chaldean Sun-god. The original form of the "T" became the emblem of the Greek - Roman Sun-god "Tammuz." The "T" became the "t" or cross that the messiah was hung on. The proper word to use is, "**stake**."

The word "angel" comes from the name of "Angelos" who was another false Greek deity associated with sun worship. The proper word to use is the Hebrew name "**Malakim**", which means, "the messenger." The **Book of Malachi** was written by a messenger of Ehyeh.

The word "grace" comes from the Greek word "charis." Charis was a Greek goddess; she was the wife of Vulcan. We get the word "Charities" from Charis's three daughters whose father was "Helios", the Greek / Roman high sun deity. The proper word to use is "**favor**."

We get the word "hell" from the name of "Hades", who was the supreme deity of the underworld for the Greeks. The proper word to use is the Hebrew word "sheol" meaning, "**the grave**."

The word "amen" is usually associated with the closing of prayer. It is an expression of firm affirmation. The word "amen" comes from the names of two gods who were known to the Egyptians in very early times as "Amen" and his consort "Ament." The proper pronunciation of the Hebrew word is, "**Aw-mien**."

The word "Sun-day" is fairly self-incriminating. Practically every ancient civilization worshiped the sun in one way or another. The Roman Emperor Constantine legislated "Sun-day" as a day of rest dedicated to the Greek and Roman Sun-god, Helios. Constantine worshipped "Christos Helios" which means, "Christ-The-True-Sun." The Roman Catholic assemblies still worship on Sunday which (as I stated earlier) is on the 1st day of the week.

Practically every protestant Christian blindly follows the Roman Catholic religion by worshiping on this false day of worship as well. "Sun-day" is a false day of worship that was legislated by a "man" instead of the Creator.

The word "Christ" is not found in the Old Testament. However, it has been inserted into the New Testament many times. Two separate incidents in the Scriptures show us evidence of the scribes altering the title of the man who was called "Christ." **(This is one of those times when we need to make sure we do not check our brains at the door.)** **John 1:41** says, "... *we have found the Messias,* which is, being interpreted, *the Christ.*" And **John 4:25** says, "... *the woman saith unto him, I know that Messias cometh,* which is called *Christ":* As you can see, in both of these verses, the man's title was originally "Messias." But after this he was always called "Christ." Do you see what the scribes have done here in these two verses? Any time that the scribes add their own words, they generally italicize their added words to let us know that they had been inserted by the writers. Do you see in your own version of Scriptures that the words; "which is being interpreted" and "which is called" are not in italics as they should have been? The proper title to use is the Hebrew word "**Messiah**" which means, "the deliverer or the savior."

The word "Christ" comes from the Greek word "Christos", meaning "anointed one." "Chrestos", as was reverenced by the Greeks and the Romans, was none other than "Osiris," who was a major sun-deity of Egypt. We need to completely eradicate and delete the word "Christ" from our vocabulary so that we will not be calling upon the name of any false pagan deity.

Finally, let's look at one last word that we need to eradicate from our vocabularies. That is the word "**bless**" or "**blessed.**" It has the e-Sword number H1288.

Let Me Count The Ways In Which We Have All Been Deceived

Blessed - H1288

בָּרַךְ

bârak

baw-rak'

A primitive root; to *kneel*; by implication to *bless* God (as an act of adoration) and (vice-versa) man (as a benefit); also (by euphemism) <u>**to *curse***</u> (God or the king, as treason):

As you can clearly see, to "bless" someone can be to favor them or it can mean to curse them. The origin of the word "blessed" has been found to have originated from <u>Germanic paganism</u>, where a sacrificial animal was killed in ritual, and it was used <u>to mark with blood</u>. One reference to this pagan practice can be found in the Scriptures. **Exodus 24:8** says, "*Moses took the blood and sprinkled it on the people and said, behold the blood of the covenant, which "Baal" has made with you concerning all of these words.*"

This is the same as when someone sneezes and some of the snot gets on you. People tend to say, "Bless you." Do you see the correlation here? This is not a good thing. The proper words to use are **"favor" or "favored."**

Every one of these previous words and terms has pagan origins and they have all been found to be directly associated to ancient Sun worship and-or the names of false pagan deities.

Now we have to ask ourselves a couple of hard questions. How did all of these false pagan words that we use in our religion come to be incorporated into our everyday language and beliefs? Was it by accident, or was it whole-heartedly intentional? I can believe that it could happen accidentally with some of these words, but not with all of them. What was the question that was asked again? **Yeremiah 8:8** asks, *"How do we say, we are wise and the instruction of Ehyeh is with us? Lo, certainly in vain made he it; for <u>the pen of the scribes</u> has made it* (the instructions) *in vain,* (worthless)."

Are you beginning to see and understand how much we have been deceived about? Are you beginning to get mad at all of the scribes and the Pharisees who have hidden all of this from you? Are you ready to learn more?

8
What Time Do You Have?

The title of this book alludes to the fact that we have all been deceived. It turns out that we have also all been deceived when it comes to the times and the seasons. This chapter may be hard to completely understand because the scribes and the Pharisees have completely manipulated time on every level. This is going to be like trying to open a 20-digit combination lock. I hope that you will be able to follow my rationalization.

It is very hard to teach someone the intricacies of something that is somewhat technical if they do not have the basics. For instance, if someone does not understand when the new day begins or when it ends, they will have a problem understanding how long a day lasts. We discovered back on page 34 that **a new day begins when the sun comes up**. We also learned **that it is night time when the stars are out**.

I have a question that I want you to ask yourselves. How many hours are there in a day? Let me guess. Did you think to yourself that there are 24 hours in a day? Let's turn to Scripture and see if it tells us how many hours are in a "day." **John 11:9** says, "*Yeshua answered, are there not twelve hours in the day*"? So right here, Yeshua himself says that there are 12 hours in a day.

Let Me Count The Ways In Which We Have All Been Deceived

Now I know what you're thinking. You are thinking; but what about the night? Well, what about the night? The first thing we need to understand is that day is day and night is night.

Now would probably be a good time for me to explain to you that Ehyeh works in cycles. There is the day and night cycle of 24 hours. Then it starts all over again. There is also the weekly cycle of seven days beginning with the 1st day of the week and ending with 7th day Sabbath. Then it starts all over again and so on.

As I was saying, Ehyeh makes an exclusive distinction between day and night. As a matter of fact, there are approximately 105 verses in Scripture where we find both the day and the night specifically mentioned.

Before we get ahead of ourselves, I want to point out that day and night have a parallel connotation. Day represents "light" while night represents "darkness." Light can also represent "wisdom", while darkness represents "ignorance."

Scripture starts off in **Genesis 1:2-5** saying, 2 *"... darkness was upon the face of the deep ... 3 and Ehyeh said, let there be light: and there was light. 4 And Ehyeh saw the light, that it was perfect: and Ehyeh divided the light from the darkness; 5 on the 1st day of creation."* I personally believe that the darkness was here first. And then Ehyeh created the light and then He divided the light from the darkness. This means that Ehyeh separated the wisdom from the ignorance on the 1st day of creation. I say that because it was not until **Genesis 1:14** that it tells us, *"Ehyeh put the luminaries in heaven on the 4th day of creation."*

> (Note): **The definition for the word "luminary" is a celestial body that puts off its own source of light. For instance, the sun has**

its own source of power, so it is self-illuminating. The same goes for all of the stars, which are also self-illuminating.

We see this correlation between light and wisdom when King Belshazzar saw the hand begin writing on the wall. When no one could be found who could read the writing, the kings' mother told Belshazzar who to call for. **Daniel 5:11** says, *"There is a man in your kingdom, in whom has the spirit of the set-apart god; and in the days of your father light and understanding and wisdom, like the wisdom of the gods, was found in him."*

I want you to go back to the original question at the beginning of this chapter. "What time do you have?" Do you have any idea where the concept of telling what time it is originated from? The **Book of Yubilees 4:17-18** tells us, 17 *"Enoch was the first among the men that were born on earth who learned writing and knowledge and wisdom, and he wrote down the signs of heaven according to the order of their months, in a book,* **18** *so that mankind might know the seasons of the years according to the order of their separate months."*

What do you believe it means when it says, "Enoch wrote down the signs of heaven"? From here we go back to **Genesis 1:14, & 16** where it says, **14** *"And Ehyeh said, Let there be luminaries in the firmament of the heaven to divide the day from the night; and let them be for signs and for seasons and for days and years:* **16** *... And Ehyeh made two great luminaries; the greater luminary to rule the day and the lesser luminary to rule the night: he made the stars also."*

Before we go any further, I need to show you how the scribes have corrupted this last sentence and have made it very confusing. To see this for yourself, you need to get your own **King James Version** of Scripture out and look at

Genesis 1:16. When you look at it you will see that the words "*he made*" are in italics, which once again, tells us that the scribes have inserted these two words. In addition to this is that the word "also" was not in the original Hebrew text either. **Verse 16** should have read like this: **Genesis 1:16** says, "*And Ehyeh made two great luminaries; the greater luminary to rule the day and the lesser luminaries to rule the night:* the stars.*"*

Do you see the difference between these two versions of this verse? Do you see the significance of this deception? To tell you The Truth, I did not see it the first time someone showed it to me.

Look at the first version again and tell me which luminary this verse is referring to when it says, "the greater luminary"? If you say that it is referring to the sun, then you are correct. Practically everyone gets that one correct.

Can you now tell me which luminary this verse is referring to when it speaks of "the lesser luminary"? Practically everyone says that this is referring to the moon. If you said it is referring to the moon, then you are incorrect.

The moon is not self-illuminating. The moon reflects the light from the sun back to the earth. When you read **Genesis 1:14-16** again, you will see that there is no mention of the moon in any of these three verses. The only things mentioned in these three verses are "*the stars*." That is because the stars are stars, and the sun is also a star.

To confirm what I am saying to you, I need for you to once again read **Genesis 1:14** which says, "*And Ehyeh said, let there be luminaries in the firmament of the* heaven to divide the day from the night; *and let them be* for signs and for seasons *and for days and years*": It says that these

75

Let Me Count The Ways In Which We Have All Been Deceived

luminaries are "to divide the day from the night." Now, answer these three questions for me.

1. Can you see the sun at night? No, you cannot see the sun at night.
2. Can you see the stars in the daylight? No, you cannot see the stars in the daylight.
3. Can you (at times) see the moon during the day as well as during the night? Yes, you can.

This essentially means that the moon does not divide the day from the night. It is actually the sun and stars which divide the day from the night. Now that we have conclusively determined that we are referring to the sun and the stars and <u>not the moon</u>, we can now learn what it means when it says, "*and let them be <u>for signs and for seasons</u>.*"

As I stated before, Ehyeh put an innumerable number of stars in the heaven on the 4th day of creation. I have been told that the sailors, who know how to read the stars, use the stars to navigate at night. Did you know that the stars were also put in the heavens for us to tell time by? Before we had any kind of written calendar, mankind was able to look up into the heavens at night and see the pictures of the constellations (Moseroth) that got their shapes by the arrangement of the stars. There are 12 months in the year and there are 12 major constellations. It is the constellations (Moseroth) that are "*<u>for signs</u>.*"

Ehyeh put the stars in the heaven so that we can know what month of the year we are in at any given time. The problem is that the majority of mankind has not been taught to study or learn to read the stars. In all reality, most of us have been persuaded not to even learn about the stars because we have been taught that it might lead us down the wrong path.

Let's look one more time at what it says about Enoch in the **Book of Yubilees. Yubilees 4:17-18** says, **17** "*Enoch was the first among the men that were born on earth who learned writing and knowledge and wisdom, and he <u>wrote down the signs of heaven</u> according <u>to the order of their months</u>, in a book,* **18** *so that mankind might know <u>the seasons of the years</u> according to <u>the order of their separate months</u>.*"

In school, I was actually taught that the sun does not move. I was taught that the earth spins on its axis and it travels around the sun. I was never taught that the sun actually travels on a path in a circle through the constellations. Did you know that Scriptures tell us all about this? **Psalms 19:1-6** tells us, "*the heavens declare the majesty of Ehyeh; and the firmament shows his handiwork.* **2** *Day after day* (the heaven) *utters speech and night after night* (the stars) *reveals knowledge.* **3** *There is no* (sound) *nor language, where their voice is not heard.* **4** *Their path has gone throughout all of the earth and their words to the end of the world. In them He has set a tabernacle for the sun,* **5** *which is as a bridegroom coming out of his chamber, which rejoices as a strong man which runs a race.* **6** *His going forth is from the end of the heaven and his circuit unto the ends of it: and there is nothing hid from the heat thereof.*"

Ehyeh put the stars all the way up in heaven so that mankind could not tamper or manipulate them. **Isaiah 55:9** says, "*For as the heavens are higher than the earth, so are my ways higher than your ways and my thoughts* (higher) *than your thoughts.*" We can all learn from these constellations even though they do not make a sound. When you step outside at night, you can look up and see the same stars and the same constellations that Ehyeh told Abraham to look up at, thousands of years ago. If you are on one side of the earth, you can look up and see and read

77

the constellations. Twelve hours later, someone who is on the opposite side of the earth can look up and see and read those same constellations. During the day, we can feel the radiating heat from the sun all around the world because it all moves in a circle.

As I stated before, Ehyeh put the stars / constellations in the heaven so that we would be able keep track of time. Enoch was the first to write all of this down in a book so that we would know how to keep track of time according to the months of the year. The problem is that many of us do not have access to the **Book of Enoch**.

At this point I will share with you another deception that you may find hard to accept. **Daniel 7:25** tells us that the beast will, *"... think to change times and laws."* Whereas **1 Thessalonians 5:1, 4, 5** says, 1 *"But of the times (signs) and the seasons, brethren, you have no need that I write unto you ... 4 For you, brethren, are not in darkness ... 5 You are all of the children of light and the children of the day: We are not of the night, nor of darkness."*

Did you know that according to both the **Book of Yubilees** and the **Book of Enoch**, there are only supposed to be 364 days in Ehyeh's calendar year? **Yubilees 6:31** says, *"You are to command the children of Yeshurun that they are to observe the years according to this reckoning, 364, days"*... And **Enoch 73:13** says, *"And the sun and the stars bring in all of the years exactly, so that they do not advance or delay their position by a single day unto eternity; but complete the years with perfect justice in 364 days."*

You will recall that I told you earlier that I believe that the scribes have taken more than just a few small pieces of specific information out of the Scriptures so that we would not know about them. I would be willing to say that this vital bit of information about the 364-day calendar is one of those important things that they took out of the Scriptures.

I can just imagine what you are thinking. You are thinking, "How can this be?" I expect that you have never heard of any of this before. The calendar that the majority of the world uses today has 365¼ days in a calendar year. So where do you suppose the extra day and a ¼ would have come from?

I have a good idea of where this additional time may have come from. Scripture tells us of two separate incidents that could possibly explain from where this extra time may have come. We find the first story in **Yoshua 10:12**, which says, "*Joshua and the children of Yeshurun were fighting the Amorites and Joshua commanded the sun to stand still.*" **Yoshua 10:13** continued, "*... So the sun stood still in the midst of heaven and hasted not to go down <u>about a whole day</u>.*" This is where the extra day may have come from.

Then do you remember when King Hezekiah got sick? **2 Kings 20:11** tells us the story of how Ehyeh made the <u>sun back up 10 degrees</u>. This is where the extra ¼ day might possibly have come from. (**As my friend likes to say; "Do not check your brains at the door." I am not telling you to believe me. I am just telling you to consider this.**) Is there even a small possibility that the scribes have put these two stories into the Scriptures in-order to justify the changing of the times and seasons?

As I shared in the story of the Roman chariots of war and the space shuttle, traditions are sometimes passed down for thousands of years. When I was young, I always watched the western shows on television. Occasionally, they would have a scene where an old Indian would say, "<u>Many moons ago</u>." This is because back then, the Indians kept track of time by the moons. It turns out that keeping

Let Me Count The Ways In Which We Have All Been Deceived

track of time by the moon goes even further back in time than before the Indians. It turns out that the Babylonians may have taught this practice to the tribe of Yahuda when they were living in captivity for 70 years.

I did not learn about this until I started studying to discover what we have been deceived about. But did you know that the people of Yahuda keep track of time according to the moon? They watch the cycles of the moon, and they say that on the night that they see the first sliver of the moon, it is considered to be the 1st day of each month.

It is fairly easy to understand why they would count their months this way. This practice has been going on since they were taken into captivity to Babylon by King Nebuchadnezzar. Another one of the principal reasons they were deceived is that the scribes have manipulated the language. It turns out that the scribes have confused the meaning of the word "month." They have changed it to mean "moon." To give you an example, I will show you how e-Sword shows us both of these words.

Job 25:5 says, *"Behold even to the moon", H3394 ..."* As you can clearly see, the word "**moon**" is number H3394.

(1) Moon - H3394

ירח

yârêach
yaw-ray'-akh
From the same as H3391; the *moon:* - moon.
This says that the word "**moon**" is also from the same as number H3391.

(2) Moon - H3391

ירח

yerach
yeh'-rakh

80

Let Me Count The Ways In Which We Have All Been Deceived

From an unused root of uncertain signification, a *lunation*, that is, *month:* - month, moon.

Now notice in this next verse that the words "new moon" has a completely different numerical value of H2320. **1 Samuel 20:18** says, *"Then Yonathan said to David, tomorrow is the **new moon**", H2320* ...

As you can see, this time the words "**new moon**" is number H2320.

New Moon - H2320

חדש

chôdesh

kho'-desh

From H2318; the *new* moon; by implication a *month:* - month (-ly), new moon.

As you can clearly see, the 1st "moon" is, "Yareach" which means, "moon", while the 2nd "moon" is, "Yerach" which means, both "**month and moon**." Then you have the "New Moon" which is "Chodesh" which also means, both "month and moon." Are you beginning to see how the scribes have corrupted all of this? This is why the Yahudians (Jews), and the Messianic groups observe and follow the moon when it comes to the beginning of each month. They are under the false belief that these two words are interchangeable. They are **not**.

Most people have no clue about this. When these individuals or groups use the moon to calculate the beginning of their months, they always have to add an additional 13th month every 3rd year. This is because each moon cycle is only 29 or 30 days long. This means that 12 full moon cycles only adds up to 354 days in a single year. This is 10 days short of the 364-day yearly cycle that Ehyeh originally established. What this means is that each year comes to an end 10 days too soon. This is why at the end of the 3rd year they are 30 days too early, which is why they need to add one additional month to make up for the 3 short years.

There is only one place in the **Scriptures** where we can find that it alludes to how many months there are in the year. To tell you The Truth, it does not specifically tell us how many months are in the year. In order for us to determine how many months there are, we have to use our brains and do some deductive reasoning to come up with the answer. **Revelation 22:2** tells us of "... *the tree of life, which bare twelve manners of fruits and yielded her fruit every month.*" Reasoning deductively, we can determine that this is telling us that there are only so many months in a year. This tree of life will only bear 12 kinds of fruit, one kind each month. This tells us that there are only 12 months in a year.

Think about this for a moment. There were 12 sons of Yacob. There are 12 gates to the New Yerusalem. There are 12 separate foundations of the city. There were 12 apostles. There are 12,000 people per tribe. There are 12 kinds of fruit. <u>**There should not be any 13th month**</u>.

As I mentioned, the reason that they have an additional 13th month every 3rd year is that the years all end ten days too early when they use the moon to determine the length of the months. Did you know that this is specifically mentioned in the **Book of Yubilees? Yubilees 6:34** tells us, "... *there will be those who will make observations of <u>the moon</u>, for this one,* (the moon) *corrupts the <u>stated times</u> and comes out earlier each year by ten days.*"

We have now decisively concluded that we are **not** supposed to use the moon to determine our months by. We

Let Me Count The Ways In Which We Have All Been Deceived

have also determined that the Yahudians and the messianic groups have been keeping track of time incorrectly for a long, long time. Now we need to learn how to tell time correctly and what we are to use for a starting point for when the New Year is supposed to actually begin. We find in **Exodus 12:1-2** that, *"Ehyeh spoke to Moses in the land of Egypt, saying,* **2** *this month shall be unto you the beginning of months: it shall be the first month of the year to you."* We have a small problem here. This still does not tell us when to begin the New Year. I would be willing to say that this is another one of those vital bits of information that the scribes have completely taken out of the Scriptures so that we would not be able to know the answer to this crucial question.

Oh, but wait a moment. Let's look at the next chapter and see if it gives us any type of clue. **Exodus 13:4** says, *"you came out in the month of Abib."* Well now we know. The 1st month of the year is the month of "Abib." So now we have to figure out what it means when we say, "the month of Abib." Let's look up this word "**Abib**" on e-Sword and discover what it means in Hebrew. Its number is H24.

Abib H24

אביב

'âbıyb

aw-beeb'

From an unused root (meaning to *be tender*); *green*, that is a young *ear* of grain; hence the name of the month *Abib* or Nisan: - Abib, ear, green ears of corn.

Before we get ahead of ourselves, we need to recognize that this still does not explain what month this is referring to. First of all, the word "Abib" is basically a characteristic of the month in question, while the word

"Nisan" is a name of Babylonian origin, so we will not be using that name.

So now, we have to ask ourselves, what time of the year would you find a new green ear of grain or corn? Deductive reasoning would bring us to conclude that this is actually speaking of <u>spring</u>. The word "Abib" is pointing us to the 1st month of spring.

I want to point out, at this time, that the calendar (The Gregorian Calendar) which the majority of the world follows today has the 1st month of the year beginning in "January" which is in the winter. Are you beginning to see how much we have been deceived about when it concerns the calendar which we have been ignorantly following? I like to challenge everyone who says, "Happy New Year" on the 1st day of January to go and wake up a bear that is hibernating and tell the bear that it is time to wake up because it is the New Year. If the bear could talk, it would tell that person to leave it alone because it is not time to wake up until springtime which is still two and a half months away.

I want to remind you one more time that **Yubilees 4:17-18** tells us, **17** *"<u>Enoch was the first among the men that were born on earth who learned writing and knowledge and wisdom,</u> and he <u>wrote down the signs of heaven</u> according <u>to the order of their months</u>, in a book,* **18** *<u>so that mankind might know the seasons of the years according to the order of their separate months.</u>"* This verse is telling us that Enoch had <u>knowledge and wisdom</u> because he was able to write down the signs in heaven and he could show mankind the order of the months and the seasons.

In the following pages there is an image of Ehyeh's 364-day calendar. As you will see, there are 12 months with 30 days to each month. 12 x 30 = 360 days. Then there

84

are also 4 individually separate *stated days* which are for the dividing of the season days. They are called "spring", "summer", "fall" and "winter." When you add these 4 stated days to the 360 days, you will get a total of 364 days in all. There are also 3 months per season. This will give you 90 days a season, plus the 1 stated dividing day which gives us a total of 91 days per season.

With 91 days per season, that divides into 13 seven-day weeks exactly. Thirteen weeks times 4 seasons make it exactly 52 complete weeks per year. This all adds up to a total of 364 days per year.

Do you remember trying to learn the complex Gregorian calendar? Some months have 31 days while some have 30 days. One has 28 days unless it is a leap year when it has 29 days. I still have to ask someone else how many days are in each month because, to tell you The Truth, I never did memorize them.

Can you imagine how easy it would have been to learn this Enochian calendar? It is so easy. **1 Corinthians 14:33** tells us, "... *Ehyeh is not the author of confusion*"... There are only 4 seasons. There are 3 months per season. There are 30 days per month. Then there is a *stated divider day* at the beginning of each quarter."

Before we get ahead of ourselves, I want to say that there are many people who call this the "Enoch Calendar", but it is in reality actually "Ehyeh's Calendar", so that is what I am calling it.

We are beginning to get closer to solving this entire thing. We just have a few more combinations that we have to unlock. Going back now to **Yubilees 4:17** again, it tells us, "*Enoch wrote down the signs of heaven.*" As I mentioned earlier, the constellations are the signs. They are depicted as seven different pictures of animals. They are the lamb, bull, crab, lion, scorpion, goat, and the fish.

85

There are five additional pictures with human figures consisting of the twins, the virgin, the false balances, the archer, and the water bearer. Each one has a name that was given to it which is associated with their image.

We know these constellations as Aries the lamb, Taurus the bull, Gemini the twins (brothers) and Cancer the crab. Then we have Leo the lion, Virgo the virgin, Libra the false scales (instruments of cruelty) and Scorpio the Scorpion. And finally, we have Sagittarius the archer, Capricorn the goat (or wolf), Aquarius the waterbearer and Pisces the fish. These names, however, are not the names which Ehyeh assigned to them.

I mentioned earlier that we can see the same stars and the same constellations that Abraham was able to look up and see way back when he was alive. **Genesis 15:5** says that Ehyeh brought Abraham outside and told him, *"now look toward heaven and tell the stars"*... This says, *"tell the stars."* This literally meant for Abraham to read the stars. You have to remember that Abraham was originally from the nation of the Chaldeans. **Daniel 5:7** tells us, *"the king cried aloud to bring in the astrologers, the Chaldeans"*... And **Daniel 5:15** says, *"now the wise men; the astrologers"*... The Chaldeans were famous throughout the land for being wise enough to be able to read the stars. Would you be surprised to learn that the stars actually tell a story? The last part of **Genesis 15:5** says, *"So shall your descendents be."*

For those of you who have read the entire **Book of Genesis**, you know that it tells of Abraham's descendants all of the way down to the 12 sons of Yacob who would eventually make up the 12 tribes of Yeshurun.

Abraham and his wife Sarah had a son named Isaac. Then Isaac and his wife Rebekah had twin sons. The youngest boy was named Yacob. Yacob ran away from his older brother Esau to his uncle Laban's home. Yacob lived with his uncle for 20 years and while he lived there, he married 4 separate wives. Those 4 wives gave Yacob a total of 12 sons and 1 daughter.

What many people do not realize is that all 4 of these wives of Yacob were idolaters. You will recall that Rachel stole her father Laban's' idols (gods) and she sat on them when Laban was searching for them. Yacob told Laban in **Genesis 31:32** that, *"with whomsoever you find your gods, let him not live"*: Remember how I said that **Proverbs 18:21** tells us, *"Life and death are in the power of the tongue."* It turns out that just four chapters later, in **Genesis 35:18** Rachel died giving birth to Benyamin.

You need to remember that Hebrew names have very significant meanings. We are now going to look at the names of each of Yacob's 12 sons and learn what each name means. As it turns out, the wives named all of the children except for the last son. It was Yacob himself who named him Benyamin.

I got the meaning of each one of the boys' names from e-Sword. **Genesis 29:32** says, *"And Leah conceived and bare a son and she called his name **Reuben**: for she said, Because Ehyeh has looked upon my affliction; for now, my husband will love me."* – Reuben: From H1121; *"see you a son";* behold a son.

Genesis 29:33 says, *"And she conceived again and bare a son; and said, Because Ehyeh has heard that I was hated, he has therefore given me this son also: and she called his name **Simeon**."* – Simeon: From H8085; *hearing;* Shimon, listen intelligently.

Genesis 29:34 says, *"and she conceived again and bare a son; and said, Now this time will my husband be joined unto me, because I have born him three sons: therefore, was his name called **Levi**."* – Levi: From H3867;

attached; to *twine*, that is, (by implication) to *unite*, to cleave, join.

Genesis 29:35 says, "*And she conceived again and bare a son: and she said, Now will I praise Ehyeh: therefore, she called his name **Yahuda**; and stopped bearing.*" – Yahuda: From H3034; *celebrated*; literally to praise, to *revere* or *worship* (with thanksgiving).

Genesis 30:5, 6 says, "*And Bilhah conceived and bare Yacob a son. And Rachel said, Ehyeh has judged me and has also heard my voice and has given me a son: therefore, she called his name **Dan**.*" – Dan: From H1777; *to judge*; to *rule*; - contend, to execute (judgment),

Genesis 30:7, 8 says, "*And Bilhah Rachel's maid conceived again and bare Yacob a second son. And Rachel said, with great wrestling's have I wrestled with my sister, and I have prevailed: and she called his name **Naphtali**.*" – Naphtali: From H6617; properly *wrestled*; a *struggle:* - with great wrestling.

Genesis 30:10, 11 says, "*And Zilpah Leah's maid bare Yacob a son. And Leah said, A troop comes, and she called his name **Gad**.*" – Gad: A primitive root (akin to H1413); to *crowd* upon, that is, luck, fortunate.

Genesis 30:12, 13 says, "*And Zilpah Leah's maid bare Yacob a second son. And Leah said, Happy am I, for the daughters will call me blessed: and she called his name **Asher**.*" – Asher: From H833; *happy*; Asher, to *be straight*, especially to *be level, right, happy*); figuratively to *prosper:* to be upright.

Genesis 30:17, 18 says, "*And Ehyeh hearkened unto Leah and she conceived and bare Yacob the fifth son. And Leah said, Ehyeh has given me my hire, because I have given my maiden to my husband: and she called his name*

Let Me Count The Ways In Which We Have All Been Deceived

Issachar." – Issachar: From H5375 and H7939; *he will bring a reward*; a benefit.

Genesis 30:19, 20 says, "And Leah conceived again and bare Yacob the sixth son. And Leah said, Ehyeh has endowed me with a good <u>dowry</u>; now will my husband dwell with me, because I have born him six sons: and she called his name ***Zebulun***." – Zebulun: From H2082; a gift, habitation; <u>exalted</u>?

Genesis 30:22-24 says, "And Ehyeh remembered Rachel and Ehyeh hearkened to her and opened her womb. And she conceived and bare a son and said, Ehyeh has taken away my reproach: And she called his name ***Yoseph***; and said, 'Ehyeh shall <u>add to</u> me another son.'" – Yoseph: Future of H3254; *let him add*.

Genesis 35:16-18 says, "And they journeyed from Bethel; and there was but a little way to come to Ephrath: and Rachel travailed, and she had hard labor. And it came to pass, when she was in hard labor, that the midwife said unto her, 'Fear not; thou shall have this son also.' And it came to pass, as her soul was in departing, (for she died) that she called his name Benoni: but his father called him ***Benyamin***." – From H1121 and H3225; *son of* (the) *right hand or righteous son*.

Below is a list of all of Yacob's sons, in the order that they were born in, beginning with Reuben, and ending with Benyamin. As I said, the definitions for the names of these 12 sons of Yacob came from e-Sword. They are as follows:

1. Reuben --------- Look a son.
2. Simeon ---------- Listen intelligently.
3. Levi ------------- Become attached.
4. Yahuda --------- To praise.

Let Me Count The Ways In Which We Have All Been Deceived

5. Dan -------------- Judge.
6. Naphtali ------- With great wrestling's.
7. Gad ------------ Fortunate (a troop).
8. Asher ---------- Become Upright / Happy.
9. Issachar -------- He will receive a reward.
10. Zebulun -------- Exalted.
11. Yoseph --------- Let him be added.
12. Benyamin ----- Child of the right hand.

We are almost there. We have just about solved this entire puzzle concerning, "What time do you have"? We go from here to **Genesis Chapter 49**. This is where Yacob is getting prepared to die and he calls all of his sons to his bedside and favors them and tells them their future. As I said, Yacob is getting ready to die and he is telling his sons a prophetic message. This means that it is actually Ehyeh who is speaking through Yacob to the 12 sons.

Ehyeh is getting ready to assign each one of the 12 sons to each of the 12 constellations (Mazzaroth). It may sound like a cliché, but Ehyeh was putting their "names in lights" on the proverbial marquee in heaven.

<u>Those of you who have studied and know the constellations will probably understand this better than those of you who have never studied the constellations before. **As a matter of fact, this was all new to me as well.**</u>

Genesis 49:1 tells us, *"Yacob called unto his sons and said, gather yourselves together, so that I may tell you what shall befall you in the last days."*

Let Me Count The Ways In Which We Have All Been Deceived

3-4 *"Reuben you are ... **as unstable as water, thou shalt not excel.**"* **Reuben was assigned to "The Water Bearer."**

5-7 *"Simeon and Levi are brethren; instruments of cruelty* (false scales) *are in their habitations. I will divide them"...* **Simeon** was assigned to the twins, "The Brothers", while **Levi** was assigned to the "False scales."

9 *"Yahuda is ... as a lion"...* **Yahuda** was assigned to "The Lion."

13 *"Zebulun shall dwell at ... sea"...* **Zebulun** was assigned to "The Fishes."

14 *"Issachar is a strong ass / bull"...* **Issachar** was assigned to "The Bull."

17 *"Dan shall be a serpent"...* **Dan** was assigned to, "The Scorpion."

19 *"Gad, a troop shall overcome him: but he shall overcome* (fortunate) *at the last."* **Gad** was assigned to, "The Archer."

20 *"... Asher his bread shall be fat, and he shall yield royal dainties."* **Asher** was assigned to "The Virgin." She is holding a stalk of wheat to make bread from.

21 *"Naphtali is a hind* (doe or lamb) *let loose"...* **Naphtali** was assigned to "The Lamb."

22 *"Yoseph ... branches run over the wall."* **Yoseph** was assigned to "The Crab." A crab has quite a few legs.

27 *"Benyamin ... a wolf":* **Benyamin** was assigned to "The Wolf."

91

Let Me Count The Ways In Which We Have All Been Deceived

Ehyeh's 364-Day Calendar Year

30 Days Per Month - 52 Weeks - 12 Months
4 Seasons - 91 Days Per Season

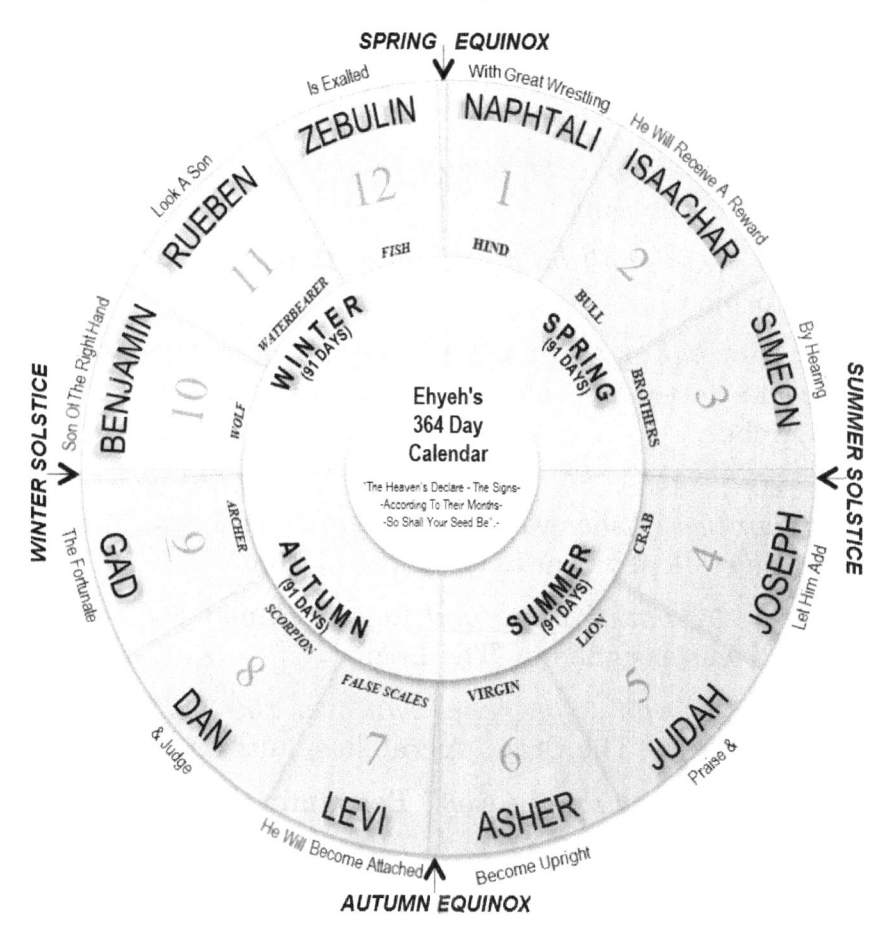

SPRING EQUINOX

- Is Exalted — ZEBULIN (12) FISH
- With Great Wrestling — NAPHTALI (1) HIND
- He Will Receive A Reward — ISAACHAR (2) BULL
- By Hearing — SIMEON (3) BROTHERS
- Let Him Add — JOSEPH (4) CRAB
- Praise & — JUDAH (5) LION
- Become Upright — ASHER (6) VIRGIN
- He Will Become Attached — LEVI (7) FALSE SCALES
- & Judge — DAN (8) SCORPION
- The Fortunate — GAD (9) ARCHER
- Son Of The Right Hand — BENJAMIN (10) WOLF
- Look A Son — RUEBEN (11) WATERBEARER

WINTER (91 DAYS) · **SPRING (91 DAYS)** · **SUMMER (91 DAYS)** · **AUTUMN (91 DAYS)**

Ehyeh's 364 Day Calendar

"The Heaven's Declare - The Signs - According To Their Months - So Shall Your Seed Be"

WINTER SOLSTICE — **SUMMER SOLSTICE**

AUTUMN EQUINOX

92

Let Me Count The Ways In Which We Have All Been Deceived

Now we can connect the 12 names of each one of Yacob's sons and the meanings of their names with the correct constellations in the order of their appearance, beginning with "The Hind or Lamb" and ending with "The Fishes."

The Moseroth:	Name:	Meaning of the Name:
1. The Hind:	Naphtali	With great wrestling
2. The Bull:	Issachar	he will receive a reward
3. The Brothers:	Simeon	by hearing intelligently
4. The Crab:	Yoseph	let him add
5. The Lion:	Yahuda	praise
6. The Virgin:	Asher	become happy / upright
7. The False Scales:	Levi	become attached
8. The Scorpion:	Dan	judge
9. The Archer:	Gad	fortunate (a troop)
10. The Wolf:	Benyamin	son of the right hand
11. The Waterbearer:	Reuben	behold a son
12. The Fish:	Zebulun	is exalted

At this point, you are probably wondering where I am going with all of this. As I previously said, Ehyeh brought Abraham outside and told him to, "Tell the stars." Ehyeh told Abraham, "so shall your seed be." Abraham could read the stars and he knew what each constellation

Let Me Count The Ways In Which We Have All Been Deceived

meant so he was able to read the message that the stars were telling him.

When you read the meanings of the names of Yacob's sons in the proper sequence, they make four separate sentences. The constellations read as follows:

1. *With great wrestling, he will receive a reward, by hearing intelligently.*
2. *Let him add praise and become upright.*
3. *He will become attached* (set-apart) *and judge the fortunate righteous child.*
4. *Look a child is exalted.*

Naphtali   Issachar   Simeon
With great effort / he will receive a reward / by listening intelligently.

Yoseph   Yahuda   Asher
Let him add / praise and / become happy.

Levi   Dan   Gad   Benyamin
He shall be set-apart / and judge / the fortunate / righteous child.

Reuben   Zebulun
Behold a child / is exalted.

So now you ask: What does all of this mean to you and me? When the Messiah was explaining how we were supposed to pray in **Luke 11:2:** he told us, *"Our Father which art in heaven, set-apart be your name. Your kingdom come. Your will (purpose) be done, <u>on earth as it is occurring in heaven</u>."* This is telling us that we are supposed to be observing the constellations and following the same calendar here on earth that Ehyeh established in heaven at the very beginning of creation. The Hebrew word for the "constellations" is the word "Mazzaroth."

Let Me Count The Ways In Which We Have All Been Deceived

Now we can connect the 12 names of each one of Yacob's sons and the meanings of their names with the correct constellations in the order of their appearance, beginning with "The Hind or Lamb" and ending with "The Fishes."

The Moseroth:	Name:	Meaning of the Name:
1. The Hind:	Naphtali	With great wrestling
2. The Bull:	Issachar	he will receive a reward
3. The Brothers:	Simeon	by hearing intelligently
4. The Crab:	Yoseph	let him add
5. The Lion:	Yahuda	praise
6. The Virgin:	Asher	become happy / upright
7. The False Scales:	Levi	become attached
8. The Scorpion:	Dan	judge
9. The Archer:	Gad	fortunate (a troop)
10. The Wolf:	Benyamin	son of the right hand
11. The Waterbearer:	Reuben	behold a son
12. The Fish:	Zebulun	is exalted

At this point, you are probably wondering where I am going with all of this. As I previously said, Ehyeh brought Abraham outside and told him to, "Tell the stars." Ehyeh told Abraham, "so shall your seed be." Abraham could read the stars and he knew what each constellation

93

Let Me Count The Ways In Which We Have All Been Deceived

meant so he was able to read the message that the stars were telling him.

When you read the meanings of the names of Yacob's sons in the proper sequence, they make four separate sentences. The constellations read as follows:

1. *With great wrestling, he will receive a reward, by hearing intelligently.*
2. *Let him add praise and become upright.*
3. *He will become attached* (set-apart) *and judge the fortunate righteous child.*
4. *Look a child is exalted.*

    Naphtali   Issachar   Simeon
With great effort / he will receive a reward / by listening intelligently.

    Yoseph   Yahuda   Asher
Let him add / praise and / become happy.

    Levi   Dan   Gad   Benyamin
He shall be set-apart / and judge / the fortunate / righteous child.

    Reuben   Zebulun
Behold a child / is exalted.

So now you ask: What does all of this mean to you and me? When the Messiah was explaining how we were supposed to pray in **Luke 11:2**: he told us, *"Our Father which art in heaven, set-apart be your name. Your kingdom come. Your will (purpose) be done, on earth as it is occurring in heaven."* This is telling us that we are supposed to be observing the constellations and following the same calendar here on earth that Ehyeh established in heaven at the very beginning of creation. The Hebrew word for the "constellations" is the word "Mazzaroth."

Question. Do you know where the word "<u>Mazel Tov</u>" comes from? It is the Hebrew expression of "Good Month." Scripture goes even further and says in **Psalms 19:11**: *"Moreover <u>by them</u> is your servant warned: <u>in keeping of them,</u>* (the ordinances) *<u>there is a great reward.</u>"*

Do you remember what I was telling you about the two-edged sword? This is essentially telling us that there is a great reward in store for those who observe this calendar. It is also a warning to those who do not live according to this calendar. We must appear before Ehyeh on the correct Sabbath days and the correct appointed days, (**feast days**).

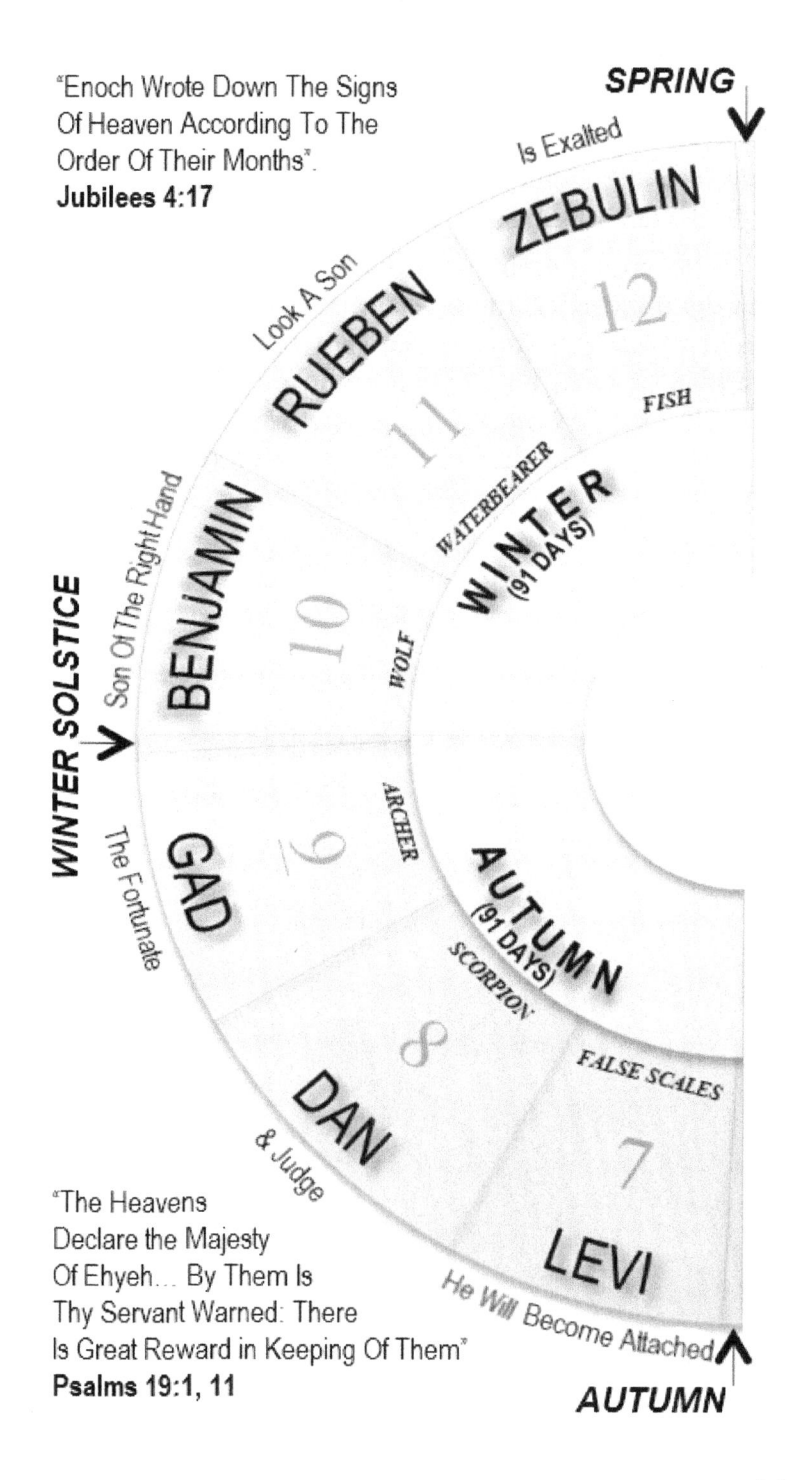

Let Me Count The Ways In Which We Have All Been Deceived

"Enoch Wrote Down The Signs Of Heaven According To The Order Of Their Months".
Jubilees 4:17

SPRING

Is Exalted

ZEBULIN

12

FISH

Look A Son

RUEBEN

11

WATERBEARER

WINTER
(91 DAYS)

Son Of The Right Hand

BENJAMIN

10

WOLF

WINTER SOLSTICE

The Fortunate

GAD

9

ARCHER

AUTUMN
(91 DAYS)

SCORPION

FALSE SCALES

& Judge

DAN

8

7

LEVI

He Will Become Attached

"The Heavens Declare the Majesty Of Ehyeh... By Them Is Thy Servant Warned: There Is Great Reward in Keeping Of Them"
Psalms 19:1, 11

AUTUMN

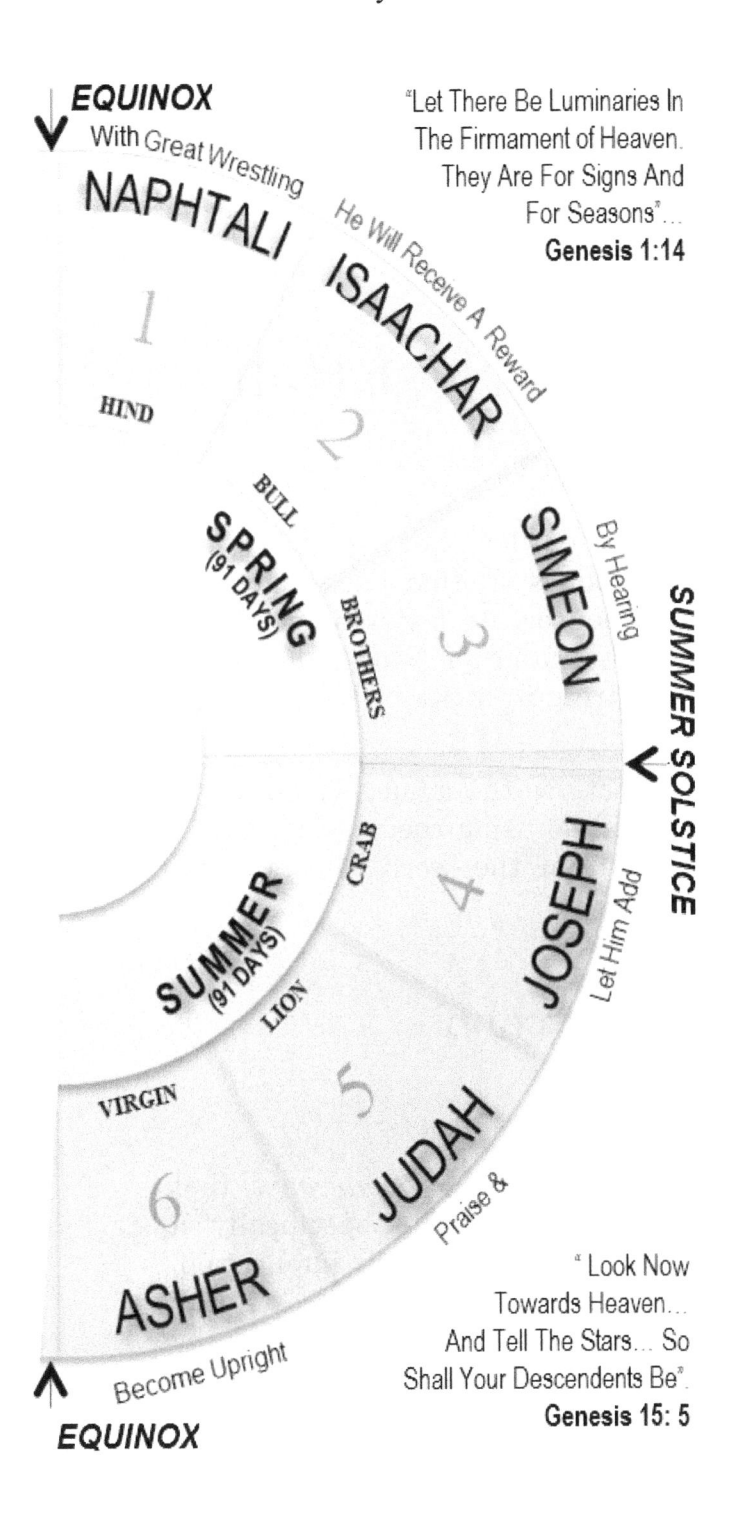

Let Me Count The Ways In Which We Have All Been Deceived

"Let There Be Luminaries In The Firmament of Heaven. They Are For Signs And For Seasons"...
Genesis 1:14

EQUINOX
With Great Wrestling
NAPHTALI
1
HIND
He Will Receive A Reward
ISAACHAR
2
SPRING (91 DAYS)
BULL
BROTHERS
SIMEON
3
By Hearing
SUMMER SOLSTICE
CRAB
JOSEPH
4
Let Him Add
SUMMER (91 DAYS)
LION
JUDAH
5
Praise &
VIRGIN
6
ASHER
Become Upright
EQUINOX

"Look Now Towards Heaven... And Tell The Stars... So Shall Your Descendents Be".
Genesis 15: 5

9
When is Your Next Holi-day?

We discovered earlier that we are not to even permit the names of other pagan deities to come out of our mouths. As I stated earlier, the word "Holy" comes from the name of "Holi", the great Hindu <u>festival</u> held in the spring in honor of Krishna, the female Sun deity.

Since we will not use the name, "Holiday" any more than we need to, I will be using the word "feasts." We get the word "festivals" from the word "feasts." This word "**feasts**" is number <u>H4150</u>.

Feasts - H4150

מועדה מעד מועד

mô'êd mô'âdâh
mo-ade', mo-ade', mo-aw-daw'

From <u>H3259</u>, properly an *appointment*, that is, a fixed *time* or season; specifically a *festival*; conventionally a *year*; by implication, an *assembly* (as convened for a definite purpose); technically the *congregation*; by extension, the <u>place of meeting</u>; also a *signal* (as appointed beforehand): - appointed (sign, time), (place of solemn) assembly, congregation, (set, solemn) feast, (appointed, due) season, solemn (-ity), synagogue, (set) time (appointed).

The word "**Moed**" means, "appointed times." Just like setting an appointment to see someone important. I will come back to this word "moed" and explain its importance later.

So, the question was, "When is your next "feast" day? Here in America we have feast days all of the time. The people who work for the government and the banks love them, because most of these feast days are paid days off. The legislatures are always introducing additional feast days so that they can honor people whom they consider special, Martin Luther King Day or Columbus Day, for instance.

The problem with this is that these feast days are supposed to be religious days. As I implied, the word "holiday" basically comes from the word "holy-day." This means that these days should actually be established by Ehyeh our Creator. So, we need to ask ourselves if days such as President's Day or Groundhog Day are days that would really qualify as feasts days.

Most Americans celebrate two individual feast days each year that they sincerely believe are actual religious feast days. The first is "Easter" and the second is "Christmas Day." What is interesting is that many people who are not even religious also celebrate these two feasts.

The name, "Easter" has its origin from the name of the Phoenician / Sidonian <u>goddess of increase</u> who went by the name of "Ashtoreth or Ishtar or Eostre". The Phoenicians lived <u>east</u> of Jordan. Ashtoreth was worshipped as the "Queen of Heaven." As I already stated,

Let Me Count The Ways In Which We Have All Been Deceived

she was worshipped as the <u>goddess of increase</u> which also refers to, "fertility."

(Note): The Easter holiday is never on the same date each year. It always falls on the first Sunday after the first full moon.

When you put all of this together, you can now understand why people still continue to get up early on <u>East</u>er Sunday and turn and face towards the <u>East</u> and have sunrise service. Then after service they go out and hunt for the (fertility) eggs which were brought by all of the fertile rabbits that <u>reproduce</u> so quickly. Rabbits can have as many as 10 to 12 liters per year. Rabbits are the ultimate emblem of reproduction. Now is when you have to ask yourself if this Easter feast is actually something that Ehyeh would sanction? No. He would not authorize it. Easter is nothing more than another false pagan festival that the Christians have been ignorantly deceived into celebrating.

Then there is Christmas Day. Christmas day originated with the celebration of the "return of the sun." As you know, the winter solstice is generally within a week of Christmas day. Christmas day is always on the 25th day of the month of December. This is the same day that the sun worshippers celebrated because the days were beginning to get longer again. At some point in time the Christians began worshiping this same day as the day of the birth of the son of the Creator. Researchers have concluded that the man called Yeshua was not actually born in December. Many Christians know this, but they still continue to celebrate this false pagan feast day.

The name, "Christmas", comes from the Catholic assembly's definition meaning <u>"Christos"</u> which means, "Christ-the-True-Sun" and <u>"mas"</u> meaning "Mass." Several books that have been written spell out all of the myths and

Let Me Count The Ways In Which We Have All Been Deceived

traditions surrounding this false festival in great detail. Neither one of these false feasts have anything to do with the true feasts of Ehyeh.

We have now determined that every one of the so called "feast days" that we in America celebrate are in fact "false feast days." So now we have to ask ourselves whether Ehyeh actually has any true feast days during which He has commanded us to present ourselves before him.

You have to remember what I said about what a feast is in Hebrew. The word "feast" actually means, "**Moed**" in Hebrew, which means, "appointed time." This is an appointed time, which was appointed by Ehyeh himself for us (mankind) to present ourselves before the Creator of this world. These are not appointments that we can just brush off and say that we will make them up later. Ehyeh, The Creator of the entire world has commanded our presence.

We can learn about the first feast that Ehyeh has commanded mankind to observe in **Leviticus 23:1-3**. It says, *"Ehyeh spoke to Moses, saying, 2 speak to the children of Yeshurun and say to them, <u>concerning the feasts of Ehyeh</u>, which you shall proclaim to be <u>set-apart</u> **<u>convocations</u>**, even <u>these are my feasts</u>. 3 Six days shall work be done, but <u>the seventh day is the Sabbath of rest</u>, a set-apart **convocation**; you shall do no work therein: it is the Sabbath of Ehyeh in all your dwellings."*

One of the main things that we pick up on in these instructions is that it says that these days are to be a "set-apart convocations."

A "convocation" is in essence, exactly the same as a feast or Moed.

This set-apart convocation is nothing short of a wedding rehearsal that the King of the earth has invited us

101

Let Me Count The Ways In Which We Have All Been Deceived

to attend. These wedding rehearsals are always at a predetermined set time.

According to e-Sword the word "**convocation**" is number H4744.

Convocation - H4744

מקרא

miqrâ'

mik-raw'

From H7121, something *called* out, that is, a public *meeting* (the act, the persons, or the palace); also, a *rehearsal:* - assembly, calling, convocation, reading.

Have you heard of the 4th **Commandment? Exodus 20:8-11** says, 8 "*remember the Sabbath day, to keep it set-apart. 9 Six days shall you labor and do all your work:* 10 *But* the seventh day *is the Sabbath of Ehyeh your Sovereign: in it you shall not do any work, you, nor your son, nor your daughter, your manservant, nor your maidservant, nor your cattle, nor your stranger that is within your gates:* 11 *For in six days Ehyeh made heaven and earth, the sea and all that in them is and rested on the seventh day: Therefore Ehyeh favored the Sabbath day and set it apart* (as special)."

As I have been trying to show you throughout this book, someone has taken great strides to deceive us about practically everything. Someone has also deceived the majority of mankind about when the 7th day Sabbath day of rest is. If you will look on practically any calendar you will see that the 7th day of the week is on "Saturday." Practically all of the Christian assembly's worship on the wrong day. They worship on the 1st day of the week instead of on the 7th day of the week.

Let Me Count The Ways In Which We Have All Been Deceived

Many Christians know they are worshiping on the wrong day, but they have never realized or understood what an important issue it is before.

There are two very strict warnings that can be found in the Scriptures that I want to show you concerning the observance of the Sabbath day. The first one can be found in **Exodus** and the second one is found in the **Book of Yubilees**.

Exodus 31:12-17 says, *"And Ehyeh spoke to Moses, saying,* **13** *you shall speak to the children of Yeshurun, saying, verily you shall strictly guard* my Sabbath *(days): Because it is a sign between me and you throughout your generations; so that you may know that I am Ehyeh who does set you apart.* **14** *Therefore you shall guard* the Sabbath *(day); because it is set-apart unto you:* Everyone that defiles the Sabbath (day) shall absolutely be put to death: *Because whosoever does any work therein, that soul shall be cut off from among his people.* **15** *Six days may work be done; but* the seventh day *is* the Sabbath *of rest, set-apart unto Ehyeh:* Whosoever does any work on the Sabbath day shall absolutely be put to death. **16** *Therefore the children of Yeshurun shall guard* the Sabbath day, *to observe* the Sabbath day *throughout their generations,* for a perpetual *(everlasting)* covenant. The Sabbath *is a sign between me and the children of Yeshurun forever: Because in six days Ehyeh made heaven and earth and on the seventh day he rested and was refreshed."*

Yubilees 2:18, 24, 25 says, **18** *"Behold, I shall separate for myself a* unique assembly of *people from among all of the* (heathen) *nations and these* (upright righteous people) *shall remember to celebrate* the (Seventh day) Sabbath *and I shall set* (those) *Yeshurun people apart to myself as a* peculiar *nation and I will set them apart unto myself as a* treasured *people and I will favor them, just as I have set* the Sabbath days *apart and I will set*

Let Me Count The Ways In Which We Have All Been Deceived

them apart to myself and thus I will favor them; and they shall be my <u>special</u> people to me and I will be their <u>King</u> to them ... **24** *All those who profane <mark>the</mark> (Sabbath) <mark>day</mark>, shall <u>definitely</u> die and all who do any kind of work on <mark>the Sabbath day</mark> shall <u>absolutely</u> die forever. So, the children <u>of the Yeshurun</u> will observe this day in all of their generations and will not be rooted <u>up</u> out of the land. Because <mark>the Sabbath day</mark> is a set-apart day;* **25** <u>*the Sabbath is*</u> *a favored day. Every person who observes and <u>guards</u> <mark>the Sabbath day</mark> and stays away from all of their work will be favored and set-apart for all of their days just as I am."* **The underlined words and words in parentheses were inserted by the author for added clarity.**

Did you happen to notice how many times it said "the Sabbath day" in these two excerpts? You will also recall that Ehyeh makes a distinction between day and night. He did not say anything at all about keeping or guarding the "Sabbath night." It turns out that the Christians are not the only people who are worshiping at the wrong time.

As I mentioned earlier, the Yahuda and Messianic assemblies begin their Sabbath worship when the sun goes down on the evening of the 6th day, and they continue their worship for an entire 24-hour period of time. They have been deceived just as much as the Christians.

As you have probably noticed, this is not a suggestion. It is a commandment. **Exodus 20:8** says for us to, *"Remember the Sabbath day, to keep it set-apart."* So, what does it mean when it says, "Remember"? It turns out that when Moses brought the children of Yeshurun out of Egypt, Ehyeh made them observe the Sabbath day when they were in the wilderness for 40 entire years. For 40 years the manna came down from heaven every morning, but on the 6th day twice as much manna came down from heaven so that they did not have to go outside and gather it on the 7th Sabbath day. There was not any manna to pick up on the 7th day.

There are 52 weeks per year. That means that we have 52 Sabbaths that are considered Ehyeh's feasts that we have been commanded to guard and observe. As a matter of fact, the first feast mentioned in **Leviticus 23:2-4** is the seventh day Sabbath.

How about it, do you suppose that there could be any more of Ehyeh's feast days that we are commanded to observe?

Before we go there, we need to look at a few more things that we have been deceived about. We will come back to that question later.

10
Where Did The Deception Begin?

By now you should be seeing that we have been deceived on practically every level. Now we want to get an idea where all of this deception started. As with any type of job or opportunity, there is a test that we all have to pass in order to succeed.

We have been taught that Ehyeh does not test mankind. But is that really true? The word "try" is used in 17 separate verses of Scripture. The word "tried" is also used in 19 separate verses of Scripture. The following four verses of Scripture use each of these words two separate times:

Yeremiah 17:10 says, *"I Ehyeh, search the heart; I <u>try</u> (test) the reins, even to give every man according to his ways and according to the fruit of his doings."*

1 John 4:1 says, *"Beloved, believe not every spirit, but <u>try</u> the spirits whether they are from Ehyeh: because many false prophets have gone out into the world.*

Daniel 12:10 says, *"Many shall be purified and made white and <u>tried</u>; but the wicked shall do wickedly: and none* *of the wicked shall understand; but the wise shall understand."*

James 1:12 says, *"Favored is the man that endures temptation: because when he is <u>tried</u>, (tested) he shall receive the crown of life, which Ehyeh has promised to them that love Him."*

As you can clearly see, Ehyeh tests every human being to see if they will obey His instructions or not. **Deuteronomy 30:19** says, *"I call heaven and earth to record this day against you, that I have set before you <u>life and death, favoring's and curses</u>: therefore, choose life, so that both you and your children may live."* As you can clearly see, it is a choice that each of us must make. We are being tested daily.

The Scriptures tell us that Eve was the first person to be deceived. **Genesis 3:1** says, *"The serpent was more subtle than any beast of the field which Ehyeh had made."* The question we have to ask ourselves is: where did this serpent come from?

(Note): This is in Genesis, which actually means the beginning. But now we are going to turn to Revelation, which is the revealing. The beginning is the end, and the end is the beginning. It is all cyclical.

Revelation 4:2, 6-8 says, *"and immediately I (John) was in the spirit: and behold, a throne was set in heaven, and one sat on the throne ... 6 ... and around about the throne, were <u>four beasts</u> full of eyes before and behind. 7 And the first beast was <u>like a lion</u> and the second beast <u>like a calf</u> and the third beast had a <u>face as of a man</u> and the fourth beast was <u>like a flying eagle</u>. 8 And <u>the four beasts had each of them six wings</u> about him; and they were full of eyes within:*

(Note): There is no mention anywhere in Scripture about any two-winged creatures besides the birds. The Scriptures only speak about two different kinds of creatures that have wings. The Cherubim have four wings, and the <u>Seraphim have six wings</u>.

Now we need to discover what these Seraphim actually are. According to e-Sword a "**Seraphim**" is number <u>H8314</u>.

<u>Seraphim - H8314</u>

שָׂרָף

śârâph

saw-rawf'

From <u>H8313</u>, *burning*, that is, (figuratively) *poisonous* (serpent); specifically, a *saraph* or symbolical creature (from their copper color): fiery (serpent), seraph.

If you allow your deductive reasoning to kick in, you will conclude that the serpent that deceived Eve was actually one of these Seraphim which was sent from the throne of Ehyeh to test Eve. I would be willing to say that it was the Seraphim with the <u>face of a man</u> that actually spoke to Eve.

I have been trying to show you how the scribes have manipulated the Scriptures, but so far, I have not made much of an issue with the Pharisees. At this point, I want to show you a couple of things that do not seem to add up when it concerns the Pharisees. As Yeshua clearly implied, the scribes and the Pharisees were working hand in hand together to deceive the people.

Exodus Chapter 2 is where we learned that both Moses' mother and father were from the tribe of Levi.

Let Me Count The Ways In Which We Have All Been Deceived

When Moses was on top of Mount Sinai for 40 days and 40 nights, Moses' brother Aaron created the golden calf for the people to worship. After Aaron had cast the golden calf, He made a proclamation to the people. **Exodus 32:4** says, *"These are your gods ... which brought you up out of the land of Egypt."*

For those of you who did not leave your brains at the door, how is it that Ehyeh chose Aaron and his sons to become the high priests? As I just showed you, it was Aaron who had made the golden calf. Then when Moses came down from the mountain where he had just received the commandment not to kill, he called for those who would stand with him. **Exodus 32:26-28** says, *"Moses stood in the gate of the camp and said, who is on Ehyeh's side? Let him come unto me. And <u>all of the sons of Levi</u> gathered themselves together unto him. And he said unto them,* **27** *Thus saith Ehyeh the Sovereign of Yeshurun, every man put his sword by his side and go in and out from gate to gate throughout the camp and slay every man his brother and every man his companion and every man his neighbor.* **28** *And the <u>children of Levi</u> did according to the words of Moses: and there fell of the people that day about three thousand men."*

So here we have Aaron who was a descendant of Levi, building this false god and then it was all of the sons of Levi who went through the camp with swords to kill about 3000 people. Is something suspicious going on here with these writings?

There is something else to look at which appears to be highly suspicious. According to Scripture, Ehyeh does not change, and He does not make mistakes. But we see here in **Numbers 3:40, 42-43,** that **40** *"Ehyeh said unto Moses, number all of the firstborn of the males of the children of Yeshurun from a month old and upward and take the number of their names.* **42** *And Moses numbered,* *as Ehyeh commanded him, all of the firstborn among the children of Yeshurun. 43 And all of the firstborn males by the number of names, from a month old and upward, of those that were numbered of them, were twenty and two thousand two hundred and threescore and thirteen, (22.273)."*

Numbers 3:41 is the verse that is suspicious because it is repeated almost word for word in **Numbers 3:45**. **Numbers 3:41** says, *"And you shall take the Levites for me **instead of** all of the firstborn among the children of Yeshurun"*. And **Numbers 3:45** says, *"Take the Levites **instead of** all of the firstborn among the children of Yeshurun"*...

It is of my personal opinion that the scribes actually inserted **verse 41** in between **verses 40** and **42**. As you can clearly see, in both **verses 41 and 45** it has the words, "**instead of**" which would imply that Ehych changed his mind.

I also believe that Ehyeh actually chose the firstborn children from each family from all 12 tribes to be his priests. But then the tribe of Levi somehow took over. Maybe it has something to do with the fact that they were the same ones who had put on their weapons and killed the 3,000 after Aaron had built the false calf/bull idol.

If we look back to the time when Yacob was favoring all 12 of his sons on his death bed, we find that Ehyeh actually cursed Simeon and Levi through Yacob. **Genesis 49:5-7** says, 5 *"Simeon and Levi are brethren; instruments of cruelty are in their habitations. 6 __O my soul, come not thou into their secret; unto their assembly, mine honor, be not thou united__: for in their anger they slew a man and in their selfwill they digged down a wall. 7 __Cursed be their anger__, for it was fierce; and their wrath, for it was cruel: I will divide them in Yacob and scatter them in Yeshurun."*

Since Yacob was getting ready to die, it was Ehyeh who was actually speaking. It was Ehyeh who said, *"O my soul, come not thou into their secret; unto their assembly, mine honor, be not thou united"*. What this is telling us is that Ehyeh did not favor Simeon or Levi. Ehyeh actually cursed the both of them. Oh, by the way, the scribes were originally from the tribe of Simeon and the Pharisees were originally from the tribe of Levi.

While we are on the subject of the Levites, let's look at a couple of other things that the Scriptures tell us about them. As I said before, Aaron was somehow chosen to be the high priest and his 3 sons were given the responsibility of maintaining and carrying the arc and the tabernacle around in the wilderness for the 40 years that they moved.

Do you recall what the **2nd Commandment** says? **Exodus 20:4-5** says, 4 *"You shall not make unto you any graven image, or any likeness of anything that is in heaven above, or that is in the earth beneath, or that is in the water under the earth: 5 You shall not bow down yourself to them, nor serve them"*.

Let's break this down and see if we can determine exactly what this is saying to us. It says, "You shall not make any carved image (idol) that looks like anything that is in heaven or on earth or in the water, which means the oceans. You shall not bow down or serve these idols."

Ehyeh commanded them not to make any type of carved image that looks like anything in heaven or on earth or in the waters, but then the Scriptures tell us that He turns around and instructed Moses to build an ark that has two gold-covered Cherubims on top of the mercy seat. Let's look at that for a moment. **Exodus 25:1, 10-11, 18-20** says, 1 "***The Lord*** *spoke to Moses, saying ...* **10** *they shall make an ark of shittim wood: The length thereof shall be two and a half cubits and the breadth thereof a cubit and a half and the height thereof a cubit and a half ...* **11** *And you shall overlay it with pure gold; you shall overlay it inside and outside and shall make a crown of gold around about on it ...* **18** <u>*And you shall make two cherubims of gold;*</u> *you shall make them of beaten work, in the two ends of the mercy seat.* **19** *Make one cherub on the one end and the other cherub on the other end: You shall make the cherubims on the two ends thereof of the mercy seat.* **20** *And the cherubims shall stretch forth their wings on high, covering the mercy seat with their wings and their faces shall look one to another; towards the mercy seat shall of the faces of the cherubims be."*

Let's back up and look at this with our eyes wide open for a moment. Aren't these Cherubim that they made to put on top of the ark images of the Malakim in heaven? Didn't we just read that we are not supposed to do this?

The sons of Aaron (the Priests) carried this ark around on their shoulders, in the wilderness, for 40 years. They put it in the tabernacle that they made which was called the "Holy of Holies." But now let's see what Amos has to say about all of this. **Amos 5:25-26** asks, 25 *"Have you offered unto me sacrifices and offerings in the wilderness for forty years, O house of Yeshurun?* **26** <u>*But you have carried the tabernacle of your god Moloch and Chiun your images, the star of your god, which you made to yourselves."*</u>

So, the question that this causes us to ask ourselves is which god was Moses talking to when he was told to build the ark with Cherubims on top of it. Could it be that the scribes are not always talking about "Ehyeh" every time we see the words, "**The LORD**"?

Let's look at another time when it says that "the LORD" spoke to Moses. **Numbers 21:6-9** says, **6** *"**the LORD** sent fiery serpents among the people, and they bit the people; and many people of Yeshurun died. 7 Therefore the people came to Moses and said, we have sinned, for we have spoken against **the LORD** and against you; pray unto **the LORD**, so that he will take away the serpents from us. 8 And Moses prayed for the people. And **the LORD** said unto Moses, make a fiery serpent and set it on a pole: and it shall come to pass, that everyone that is bitten, when he looks upon it, shall live. 9 And Moses made a serpent of brass and put it upon a pole, and it came to pass, that if a serpent had bitten any person, when he looked at the serpent of brass, he lived."*

There is something very uncharacteristic of Ehyeh going on here. First of all, Ehyeh tells us in the **2nd Commandment** not to make any images, but then He turns around and tells Moses to make a serpent of brass so that the people will be healed when they look toward it. Today, you can see this same image at practically ever Doctor and Dentists office.

Now that we have had our eyes opened, we can clearly see that this was not Ehyeh who was telling Moses to make an image of a serpent and put it on a pole. Maybe we should insert the name, "Baal" in the places where it said; "the LORD."

Before we move on to another topic, let's back up one more time and look inside this tabernacle that the children of Yeshurun made to contain this so-called "Holy of Holies." This was the room where they placed the ark of the testimony that had the Cherubims on top of the mercy seat. The priests also did all of their sacrificial services on the altar of sacrifice, (slaughtering) which was in the outer court yard.

We also find that when they were building the tabernacle, the people were told in **Exodus 26:1** to "*make the tabernacle with ten curtains of fine twined linen and blue and purple and scarlet: You shall make them with Cherubims of cunning work.*" This means that there were pictures of Cherubim embroidered into the curtains which hung around the "Holy of Holies" room. As I mentioned before, didn't Ehyeh command the people not to make images like this to worship? The High Priest was the only person who was allowed into this room. It was in this room that he was supposedly speaking to Ehyeh. Was Amos saying that the High Priest was, in reality, not speaking to Ehyeh at all? Maybe it was another false deity.

We have to remember that there is only one Sovereign Creator who created the entire world and all of its inhabitants. All others are false deities. Whether they really exist or if they are imaginary, they are all false deities.

We have to realize who it is that is influencing our minds and our actions. Apparently, Moses was not always able to distinguish who was speaking to him either. For you and me to know who is speaking to us, we need to

Let Me Count The Ways In Which We Have All Been Deceived

know and understand the true character of Ehyeh. We will get more into that a little while later.

There are at least two other times when we see that the scribes have used the name, "The LORD", where it should not have been put there.

Shortly after Moses met Ehyeh on top of Mount Horeb, He told Moses to return to Egypt to deliver His people from under Pharaoh's taskmasters. Scripture tells us in **Exodus 4:20, 24** that, **20** *"Moses took his wife, Zipporah and his sons and put them on a donkey and they returned to the land of Egypt ... 24 And it came to pass by the way in the inn, that "the LORD" met him and sought to kill him."* **Exodus 4:25-26** goes on to say; **25** *"Then Zipporah took a sharp stone and cut off the foreskin of her son and cast it at his feet and said, Surely a bloody **husband** art you to me. 26 So he let him (Moses) go: then she said, a bloody **husband** you are, because of the circumcision."*

Something seems somewhat irregular about this entire thing. First of all, it says that Ehyeh sent Moses to Egypt, but then it says that **"the LORD"** sought to kill him.

To understand this, we need to understand that Moses's wife Zipporah was the daughter of Reuel / Jethro, who was the Priest of Midian. They worshiped false gods rather than Ehyeh. This does not give much detail, but apparently Zipporah knew that this false god wanted blood. It said that as soon as Zipporah had thrown the foreskin of her son at his feet, he let Moses go. Then Zipporah said, "What a bloody '**husband**' you are"...

Once again, if we allow our deductive reasoning to kick in, we come to the conclusion that the bloody husband who tried to kill Moses was in actuality "Baal." **Yubilees 48:2** actually tells us, *it was "Prince Mastema" who tried to kill Moses at the inn."*

115

Let Me Count The Ways In Which We Have All Been Deceived

As you can see after we have done our research, it was not Ehyeh who tried to kill Moses. It was "**Baal**" or "**Mastema**" who was also called "The LORD."

According to e-Sword the word "**husband**" has at least three separate meanings. The one that makes more sense here is number H1167.

Husband - H1167

בעל

ba'al

bah'-al

From H1166; a *master*; hence a *husband*, or (figuratively) *owner* (often used with another noun in modifications of this latter sense: - + archer, + babbler, + bird, captain, chief man, + confederate, + have to do, + dreamer, those to whom it is due, + furious, those that are given to it, great, + hairy, he that hath it, have, + horseman, husband, lord, man, + married, master, etc.

I will now show you one final time when the words "the LORD", was put into the Scriptures when it was not supposed to be there. As many of you know, many of the books of Scripture were written by different writers. Several times the story is told by one writer and then later on the same story is told by another writer. The next two verses of Scripture are talking about the same story but if you pay close attention you will see that some of the details have changed. **1 Samuel 24:1** says, "*And again the anger of "the LORD" was kindled against Yeshurun and he moved David against them to say, go, number Yeshurun and Yahuda.*" But now notice what **1 Chronicles 21:1** says, "*and "Satan" stood up against Yeshurun and provoked David to number Yeshurun.*" As we can clearly see, it was not Ehyeh who was telling David to number his armies. Just as Moses had a hard time telling who he was obeying, King David also had a hard time telling who was speaking to him as well.

The thing that we need to learn from this is that just because it says, "The LORD," it does not necessarily mean that this is always talking about Ehyeh the Creator. There is a good possibility that this speaking of another false deity.

Let Me Count The Ways In Which We Have All Been Deceived

11
Break Down Their Images

When I was a young boy, I remember asking someone why most of the assembly buildings had steeples on top of their roofs. The answer that I got at the time seemed to make sense. They said that is where they put the bell. Later on, I noticed that the majority of the steeples did not have a bell in them, so that got me to questioning the answer that I had previously heard before. It turns out that the steeples have been erected on top of the assembly buildings ever since they began to build tabernacles. If you will notice, you basically only see steeples on buildings that are places designated as places of worship. A steeple is a symbol for a place of worship, so it is, in fact, a religious symbol of worship.

The more you study, the more you learn that the original theme behind the erection of a steeple is that it originated from the pagan worship of the sun god. The sun god was worshiped because it provided heat and was a source of life. The image of the steeple is generally a four-sided image that is broad at the base and comes to a point at the top.

The steeple is nothing less than a male phallus which was set up as a symbol of sexual fertility that is pointed towards the sun. It is an obelisk. One source

Let Me Count The Ways In Which We Have All Been Deceived

defines the "obelisk" as a slender, four-sided, tapering monument dedicated to the sun god of either Amon or Ra and symbolic of the erect penis. The obelisk symbolized the sun god "Ra." It was also thought by many that <u>the gods existed within the structure</u>. A perfect example of how the people believed that their gods lived inside the obelisk can be found in the totem poles that the Alaskan Eskimos have built in honor of their gods.

The steeple is directly associated with sun worship. In the center of the Vatican a stone image is set up which, if you look closely, you can see is actually used as a sun dial. A stone or masonry image called the Washington Monument has been set up in Washington, DC. You can see this image portrayed in practically every major television show that is set in Washington, DC. An obelisk called Cleopatra's Needle has also been set up in New York's Central Park.

You may be wondering what my point is in telling you all of this about the obelisks. Below is a list of 15 verses of Scripture that deal specifically with this topic.

- **Exodus 23:24** says, *"Thou shall not bow down to their gods, nor serve them, nor do after their works: but thou shall utterly overthrow them and quite <u>break down their images</u>."*
- **Exodus 34:13** says, *"But you shall destroy their altars, <u>break their images</u> and cut down their groves":*
- **Leviticus 26:1** says, *"You shall make you no idols nor <u>graven image</u>, neither rear you up a <u>standing image</u>, neither shall you set up any <u>image of stone</u> in your land, to bow down unto it: for I am Ehyeh your Mighty One."*
- **Deuteronomy 7:5** says, *"But thus shall you deal with them; you shall destroy their altars and <u>break down*

119

Let Me Count The Ways In Which We Have All Been Deceived

their images and cut down their groves and *burn their graven images with fire*.

- **Deuteronomy 12:3** says, *"And you shall overthrow their altars and break their pillars and burn their groves with fire; and you shall hew down the graven images of their gods and destroy the names of them out of that place."*

- **2 Kings 3:2** says, *"And he wrought evil in the sight of Ehyeh; but not like his father and like his mother: for he put away the image of Baal that his father had made."*

- **2 Kings 10:27** says, *"And they broke down the image of Baal and broke down the house of Baal and made it a draught house unto this day."*

- **2 Chronicles 14:3** says, *"For he took away the altars of the strange gods and the high places and broke down the images and cut down the groves":*

- **2 Chronicles 31:1** says, *"Now when all this was finished, all Yeshurun that were present went out to the cities of Yahuda and broke the images in pieces and cut down the groves and threw down the high places and the altars out of all Yahuda and Benyamin, in Ephraim also and Manasseh, until they had utterly destroyed them all. Then all of the children of Yeshurun returned, every man to his possession, into their own cities."*

- **Yeremiah 43:13** says, *"He shall break also the images of Bethshemesh, that is in the land of Egypt; and the houses of the gods of the Egyptians shall he burn with fire."*

- **Micah 5:13** says, *"Your graven images also will I cut off and your standing images out of the midst of you; and thou shall no longer worship the work of thine hands."*

Let Me Count The Ways In Which We Have All Been Deceived

- **Isaiah 17:8** says, *"And he shall not look to the altars, the work of his hands, neither shall respect that which his fingers have made, <u>either the groves, or the images</u>."*

- **Isaiah 27:9** says, *"By this therefore shall of the iniquity of Yacob be purged; and this is all of the fruit to take away his sin; when he makes all of the stones of the altar as chalkstones that are beaten in sunder, <u>the groves</u> <u>and images shall not stand up</u>."*

These two pictures of several Eskimo totem poles show the images of many of their deities.

So, what should we conclude from all of this information? By deductive reasoning, we must conclude that the obelisks that have been set up all around the world were originally thought to be places where the gods of the pagan nations resided. If that is in fact the case, what exactly does that mean when it comes to the steeple that is on top of your assembly building? In today's society we cannot break down or burn these pillars or images, but we can sure refuse to enter into a place of worship that has one of these images on top of the building.

Let Me Count The Ways In Which We Have All Been Deceived

Do you see the male phallus in the very center of the Vatican?

The obelisk of RA, the sun deity, was set up in the center of the sun disk in St. Peter's Square in Vatican City.

Let Me Count The Ways In Which We Have All Been Deceived

The Washington Monument in Washington DC.

Cleopatra's Needle (In New York's Central Park).

Let Me Count The Ways In Which We Have All Been Deceived

    The six preceding photos are just a few examples of the various obelisks that you can find in any town in America. To see the image of an obelisk or sacred pillar up close and personal, just go around the town that you live in and check out all of the male phallus on top of your own personal assembly buildings.

12
The Central Theme Of The Scriptures

One of the principle themes or mysteries of Scripture is the planting of the garden. **Ehyeh made the** earth (land) first. Then He provided a water source (the upper firmament) to water the land. Then he planted the grass and the herbs and the trees. Then He put all of the animals on the earth and in the sea. The last thing that Ehyeh did was to make mankind from the dust of the earth to work in His new garden.

A hundred years ago, everyone in the world would have understood all of the words listed below because everyone planted and harvested their own food. This would apply to practically everyone. This is why Ehyeh would have used these words as a backdrop for his Scriptures.

The following is a short list of some of the words that are used over and over in the Scriptures. The (0) is the number of times these words are mentioned in the Scriptures.

- Earth – **Genesis 1:12** says, *"And the **earth** brought forth grass and herbs yielding seed after his kind and the tree yielding fruit,* *whose seed was in itself, after his kind: and Ehyeh saw that it was good."* (906 times)

- Water – **Genesis 2:10** says, *"And a river went out of Eden to **water** the garden; and from there it was parted and became into four heads."* (363 times)

- Till – **Genesis 2:5** says, *"And every plant of the field before it was in the earth and every herb of the field before it grew: for Ehyeh had not caused it to rain upon the earth and there was not a man to **till** the ground."* (3 times)

- Seed – **Genesis 1:11** says, *"And Ehyeh said, Let the earth bring forth grass, the herbs yielding **seed** and the fruit trees yielding fruit after his kind, whose **seed** is in itself, upon the earth: and it was so."* (254 times)

- Plant – **Psalms 107:37** says, *"And sow the fields and **plant** vineyards, which may yield fruits of increase.* (41 times)

- Sow – **Genesis 47:23** says, *"Then Yoseph said unto the people, behold, I have bought you this day and your land for Pharaoh: Lo, here is seed for you and you shall **sow** the land."* (37 times)

- Soil – **Ezekiel 17:8** says, *"It was planted in a good **soil** by great waters, so that it might bring forth branches and so that it might bear fruit, so that it might be a goodly vine."* (1 time)

- Garden – **Genesis 3:8** says, *"And they heard the sound of Ehyeh walking in the **garden** in the cool of the day: and Adam and his wife hid themselves from the presence of the*

*Ehyeh among the trees of the **garden**."* (47 times)

- Wheat – **Genesis 30:14** says, *"And Reuben went in the days of **wheat** harvest and found mandrakes in the field and brought them unto his mother Leah. Then Rachel said to Leah, give me, I pray to you, (some) of your son's mandrakes.* (51 times)

- Barley – **Ruth 1:22** says, *"So, Naomi returned and Ruth the Moabitess, her daughter in law, with her, which returned out of the country of Moab: and they came to Bethlehem in the beginning of the **barley** harvest."* (35 times)

- Bread – **Genesis 3:19** says, *"In the sweat of your face shall you eat bread, until you return to the ground; for out of it were you taken for dust you are and unto dust you shall return.* (330 times)

- Tares – **Matthew 13:36** says, *"Then Yeshua sent the multitude away and went into the house: And his disciples came to him, saying, declare to us the parable of the **tares** of the field."* (8 times)

- Trees – **Genesis 3:8** says, *"And they heard the sound of Ehyeh walking in the garden in the cool of the day: and Adam and his wife hid themselves from the presence of Ehyeh among the **trees** of the garden."* (136 times)

- Grass – **Genesis 1:11** says, *"And Ehyeh said, let the earth bring forth **grass**, the herbs yielding seed and the fruit trees yielding fruit after his kind, whose seed is in itself, upon the earth: and it was so."* (56 times)

Let Me Count The Ways In Which We Have All Been Deceived

Vineyard – **Genesis 9:20** says, *"And Noah began to be a husbandman and he planted a **vineyard**."* (59 times)

- Grapes – **Genesis 40:10** says, *"And in the vine were three branches: and it was as though it budded, and her blossoms shot forth; and the clusters thereof brought forth ripe **grapes**."* (33 times)

- Winepress – **Isaiah 5:2** says, *"And he fenced it in and gathered out the stones thereof and planted it with the choicest vines and built a tower in the midst of it and also made a **winepress** therein: and he looked that it should bring forth grapes and it brought forth wild grapes."* (14 times)

- Threshing – **1 Chronicles 21:20** says, *'and Ornan turned back and saw the angel; and his four sons with him hid themselves. Now Ornan was **threshing** wheat."* (10 times)

- Field – **Genesis 2:19** says, *"And out of the ground Ehyeh formed every beast of the **field** and every fowl of the air; and brought them to Adam to see what he would call of them: and whatsoever Adam called every living creature, that was the name thereof."* (266 times)

- Fruit – **Genesis 1:29** says, *"And Ehyeh said, behold, I have given you every herb bearing seed, which is upon the face of all of the earth and every tree in the which is the **fruit** of a tree yielding seed; to you it shall be for food."* (184 times)

Let Me Count The Ways In Which We Have All Been Deceived

- Herb – **Genesis 2:5** says, *"And every plant of the field before it was in the earth and every **herb** of the field before it grew: for Ehyeh had not caused it to rain upon the earth and there was not a man to till the ground."* (37 times)

- Pulse – **Daniel 1:12** says, *"Prove your servants, I beseech you, ten days; and let them give us **pulse** (vegetables) to eat and water to drink."* (3 times)

- Grafted in – **Romans 11:17** says, *"And if some of the branches be broken off and you, being a wild olive tree, were **grafted in** among them and with them partake of the root and the fatness of the olive tree."* (4 times)

- Dirt – **Isaiah 57:20** says, *"But the wicked are like the troubled sea, when it cannot rest, whose waters cast up mire and **dirt**."* (3 times)

- Clay – **Daniel 2:34** says, *"Thou watched till a stone was cut out without hands, which smote the image upon his feet that were of iron and **clay** and broke them to pieces."* (30 times)

- Pot – **2 Kings 4:2** says, *"And Elisha said to her, what shall I do for you? Tell me, what have thou in the house? And she said, thine handmaid has not anything in the house, save a **pot** of oil."* (20 times)

- Vessel – **2 Kings 4:6** says, *"And it came to pass, when the vessels were full, that she said unto her son, bring me yet another **vessel**. And he said to her, there are not any more **vessels**. And the oil stayed."* (41 times)

Let Me Count The Ways In Which We Have All Been Deceived

- Root – **Psalms 80:9** says, *"Thou prepared room before it and didst cause it to take deep **root** and it filled the land."* (43 times)

- Branch – **Job 8:16** says, *"He is green before the sun and his **branch** shot forth in his garden."* (34 times)

- Harvest – **Genesis 8:22** says, *"While the earth remains, seed-time and **harvest** and cold and heat and summer and winter and day and night shall not cease."* (51 times)

- Fallow Ground – Yeremiah 4:3 says, *"For thus saith Ehyeh to the men of Yahuda and Yerusalem, break up your **fallow ground** and do not sow among thorns."* (2 times)

- Gather – **Genesis 6:21** says, *"And thou take unto you from all food that is eaten, and thou shall **gather** it to you; and it shall be for food for you and for them."* (158 times)

- Pluck up – **Ecclesiastes 3:2** says, *"A time to be born and a time to die; a time to plant and a time to **pluck up** that which is planted."* (29 times)

- Reap – **Job 24:6** says, *"They **reap** every one his corn in the field: and they gather the vintage of the wicked."* (31 times)

- Sickle – **Deuteronomy 16:9** says, *"Seven weeks shall thou number unto you: begin to number the seven weeks from such time as thou begin to put the **sickle** to the corn."* (11 times)

- Mustard seed – **Luke 17:6** says, *"And Meshiach said, if you had faith as a grain of*

***mustard seed**, you might say to this sycamore tree, be thou plucked up by the root and be thou planted in the sea; and it should obey you."* (5 times)

- Ground – **Genesis 2:6** says, *"But there went up a mist from the earth and watered the whole surface of the **ground**."* (188 times)

Can you think of any more words that are associated with the garden that I may have missed, which should be added to this list?

13
Circumcision On The 8th Day

Have you ever met someone who likes to lie or embellish his stories practically every time he opens his mouth? The problem that we have with people like this is that they have just enough truth in their story to make it sound believable. However, once you have gotten to know that person, you have learned to be on your guard, and you know not to believe everything that they have to say.

I hope that by this time you have come to the conclusion that practically everything the scribes have written has some truth to it, while at the same time, the story also has a false twist or two imbedded within that same story.

The **Book of Genesis** tells us of the beginning and the book of Revelation tells us about the end. We learn in Revelation that a city called the New Yerusalem will one day come down from heaven and all Yeshurun will be able to live there.

People have been waiting for that event for hundreds and hundreds of years now. Everyone wants to dwell in that majestic city. Everyone wants to still be alive when this most important event happens. But then again, billions of people who died and were buried also wanted to see this event happen in their lifetimes.

2 Peter 3:8 says, *"beloved, be not ignorant of this one thing, that one day is with Ehyeh as a thousand years and a thousand years as one day."* As you know, Ehyeh works in weekly cycles of 7 days per week. Then the week starts all over again. When you use the day for a thousand-year equation (1 day = 1,000 years) you will come to understand that 7 days of Ehyeh's week works out to equal 7,000 years. Then the time starts over again. So, this means that the 1st day of the new week would also actually be considered the metaphorical 8,000th year. Are you following what I am trying to tell you? I hope that you comprehend this, because you need to completely understand this for the rest of this to make sense.

As I was saying, we are actually talking about the 8th day. Scripture tells us that we must be circumcised on 8th day / 8,000th year. According to **Genesis 17:10-14**, we learn that "Abraham was told to circumcise the foreskin of his flesh and the foreskin of his son Ishmael and the foreskins of all his men in order for them to become a part of Ehyeh's family." After this, all newborn boys were to be circumcised on the 8th day. We find that later on in **Genesis 21:4** that, *"Abraham circumcised his son Isaac being eight days old, as God had commanded him."* Back on page 115 we saw that Zipporah said that "the LORD" (Mastema) who had tried to kill Moses was a bloody husband or god because of the circumcision.

Once again, we need to understand who it was commanding Abraham to cut off the foreskin of their flesh. Was it Ehyeh or was it another false god?

The statement was made earlier that we need to have a renewing of our minds. These men were thinking literally. When they were told that they had to cut off their

Let Me Count The Ways In Which We Have All Been Deceived

foreskins on the 8th day, the only thing that made sense to them was to cut off the foreskin of their penis.

However, if you will allow yourselves to comprehend what I am trying to share with you, I ask that you consider the following. The following 3 verses will clarify exactly what Ehyeh really wanted from his people. **Deuteronomy 10:16** says, "*<u>Circumcise therefore the foreskin of your heart</u> and be no more stiff-necked.*" **Deuteronomy 30:6** says, "*And Ehyeh your Sovereign will <u>circumcise your heart and the hearts of your descendents</u>, to love Ehyeh you're Sovereign with all your heart and with all your soul, so that you may live.*" And **Yeremiah 4:4** says, "*<u>Circumcise yourselves to Ehyeh</u> and <u>take away the foreskin of your hearts</u>, you men of Yahuda and inhabitants of Yerusalem*"...

Are you beginning to see it now? Do you understand now that Ehyeh does not want anyone to cut off the foreskin of their penis? What Ehyeh wants is for us all, men and woman alike, to cut the foreskins of our hearts and allow our mind-sets to be changed. If we will do this, then we will be permitted to enter into the New Yerusalem at the beginning of the new week which will occur on the metaphorical 8th day / 8,000th year.

Cutting the foreskin of your heart is metaphorical. It is not literal. There will not be any blood spilled on the ground. Ehyeh does not require blood as the scribes and Pharisees have erroneously led us to believe. What Ehyeh does require from us is obedience to his instructions.

14
They Have Broken The Everlasting Covenant

At the beginning of this book, I told you that you would probably get mad once you have read and learned some of the things that I have written about. I was absolutely livid when I first learned some of these things. Here I was trying to learn The Truth, but none of the preachers were telling The Truth. As **Yeremiah 16:19** says, *"...the heathen shall come unto you from the ends of the earth and shall say, surely our fathers have inherited lies, vanity and things wherein there is no profit."* As I said before, the preachers cannot teach what they do not know. This verse says that *"we have inherited lies."* This means that we have all grown up learning things that were not true. This next subject may upset you the most. I for one did not want to hear it. I did not want to accept it because if it were true, it would mean, more than any other thing, that I would have to alter my lifestyle. The longer I was able to put off hearing about this subject, the longer I could go without making any kind of life-altering changes. Provided, of course, that there was any truth to it at all.

As I mentioned before, **Proverbs 18:13** tells us, *"an individual who makes a final decision about anything* *without listening to all of the facts is a fool and this conclusion will bring shame to that individual."* The problem that many of us have is that we want to hear The Truth, but as Jack Nickolas stated in the movie *A Few Good Men,* "You can't handle The Truth." We want to hear The Truth but, most of us cannot handle The Truth.

Isaiah 24:5 says, *"the earth also is defiled under the inhabitants thereof, because they have transgressed the laws, changed the ordinance, <u>broken the everlasting covenant.</u>"*

So, the question is what exactly is "**the everlasting covenant**"? For us to determine what has been broken, we have to understand what a "covenant" actually is. This word is not used outside of a religious context very often. **Wikipedia** says, "A covenant is a solemn agreement to engage in or refrain from a specified action. It is commonly found in religious contexts, where it refers to sacred agreements between the Almighty Creator and human beings." According to **Webster's New World Dictionary,** the word "covenant" is an agreement. The first of six specific definitions says that it is "a binding and solemn agreement to do or keep from doing a specified action." Definitions **#5** and **#6** add to the specifics of what a covenant is. Number 5 says, "Law a) a formal, sealed contract, b) a clause of such a contract, c) a suit for damages for violation of such a contract. Definition **#6** is "Theo: the promise made by the Almighty Creator to mankind, as recorded in the Scriptures."

When you take into consideration the specifics of what a covenant actually is, you have to conclude that it is not just an agreement between two separate entities. It is, in effect, a binding contract which has serious consequences. If one of the two separate parties of the covenant does not hold up their end of the contract, they are subject to penalties for violating the agreement.

Let Me Count The Ways In Which We Have All Been Deceived

When it comes to a covenant which is made between mankind and the Almighty Creator of the world, it is mankind who are the ones who do not hold up to their end of the covenant. We have to realize that Ehyeh does not need anything from mankind. Mankind is completely and wholeheartedly dependent upon Ehyeh for everything we have, including the breath that we breathe, in order to continue living.

According to Scripture, the first covenant or agreement that Ehyeh made with mankind was in the Garden of Eden. Ehyeh told Adam and Eve that they could eat from any tree in the garden except from the tree of good and evil. Adam and Eve would have lived forever if they had strictly adhered to the specific instructions of this covenant. This covenant that Ehyeh made with Adam and Eve was not like a contract we might make today with a banker, for instance, where we have to pay a ten-percent penalty if we are late. This covenant had one specific penalty for failing to follow and obey the strict, specific instructions. That penalty was death. When Adam and Eve ate from the tree of good and evil, they broke the covenant. This covenant was no longer binding upon Ehyeh because– no pun intended– the other party, Adam and Eve, did not live up to their part of the agreement.

This covenant that Ehyeh made with Adam and Eve was broken. The covenant was broken just like a glass that is shattered when it hits the floor. It could not be fixed. No matter how much Adam and Eve regretted their decision to eat from the tree of good and evil, Adam and Eve could not convince Ehyeh to change his mind and permit them to continue living. Scripture tells us that Ehyeh does not change.

In order for mankind to have a chance of living, Ehyeh had to renew his covenant with mankind. The original covenant with Adam and Eve specifically dealt with what they were and were not allowed to eat. One has to wonder whether the renewed covenant would also be associated with things that we can and cannot eat. As I said before, I have always wondered what specifically the everlasting covenant was.

We already have a clue that the everlasting covenant is connected with what we can and cannot eat. We find that the first time Ehyeh mentions food is in **Genesis 1:29** where it says, *"Ehyeh said, see, I have given you every herb bearing seed, which is upon the surface of all of the earth and every tree, in which is the fruit of a tree yielding seed; to you it shall be **for meat**."* **Whoa, stop the presses again.** Do you see what the scribes have done to this verse? They have corrupted this verse. Please read this verse one more time, but this time, insert the word "food" instead of "meat." The **King James Version of Scripture** says, "Meat", whereas most other versions of Scripture say, "food." Please answer this question for me. What do fruits and vegetables have to do with "meat"? Fruits and vegetables come from the ground. We get them from the garden.

Right here we see that Ehyeh has given us the fruit trees and the vegetables to eat. Not only that, but we also get the grain crops, from which we can make flour to make different kinds of breads. We have wheat bread, rye bread, corn bread and barley bread among many others. Bread is the main staple of mankind's diet. Then there is also every kind of bean you can think of. Scripture goes on to tell us that Ehyeh has given the same thing to the animals of the earth to eat. **Genesis 1:30** says, *"And to every beast of the earth and to every bird of the air and to every thing that creeps upon the earth, wherein there is life, I have given every green herb for food: and it was so."* So Ehyeh originally gave mankind **and** all animal life vegetation to eat.

Let Me Count The Ways In Which We Have All Been Deceived

We learned that Ehyeh created the great whales and the fish of the sea and the birds of the air on the 5th day of creation. I would like to ask you to pay close attention to how these next two verses are structured, because we will come back to them later. **Genesis 1:20, 21 says, 20** *"Ehyeh said, let the waters bring out abundantly <u>the moving (swarming) creatures</u> that have life and birds that may fly above the earth in the open firmament of heaven. 21 Ehyeh created great whales and <u>every living creature that moves</u> (swarms), which the waters brought out abundantly, after their kind and every winged bird after his kind: Ehyeh saw that it was good."* So far, we have two types of animals mentioned: the animals of the water (the fish) and the animals of the air (the birds).

On the 6th day, Ehyeh created four more types of animals. **Genesis 1:24-26 says, 24** *"Ehyeh said, let the earth bring forth the living creature after his kind, <u>livestock</u> and <u>creeping things</u> and <u>beasts</u> of the earth after his kind: and it was so. 25 Ehyeh created the beast of the earth after his kind and livestock after their kind and everything that creeps upon the earth after his kind: Ehyeh saw that it was good. 26 Ehyeh said; let us make <u>mankind</u> in our image, after our likeness":*

The livestock would be the domesticated animals, such as the cattle, sheep, goats, horses. The creeping things would be those animals that slither and crawl, such as the snakes and lizards and alligators (the reptiles). The beasts of the earth would be the undomesticated animals, such as the lions and rhinos and monkeys and giraffes. The last beast that Ehyeh created was mankind.

Did you know that Scripture tells us that mankind is to have dominion over all of the animals? **Genesis 1:26** says, *"Ehyeh said let us make mankind in our image, after our likeness: and <u>let them have dominion</u> over the fish of the sea and over the birds of the air and over the livestock* *and over all* (of the beast) *the earth and over every creeping thing that creeps* (the reptiles) *upon the earth.* The word "dominion" has two different definitions. In one sense, it means, "to dominate and rule over." In another sense, it means, "to take care of and provide for." I believe that the context of **verse 26** infers that this second definition was the original intention.

Today, society has the first definition in mind. We regularly hear in the news about people being arrested because they have animals that are found to be malnourished or cruelly treated and or are in need of medical attention. Millions of people get hunting licenses every year so that they can go get a trophy to hang on their walls at home. Millions of animals are shot and killed just for sport and then many of them are left where they fell because they are just too heavy to carry back to the hunter's truck.

Did you know that, according to Scripture, mankind does not have anything special over the animals? **Ecclesiastes 3:18-20** says, **18** *"I said in my heart, concerning the matter of the descendents of men; Ehyeh selects them, so as to see that they themselves are beasts.* **19** *For the event of the children of men is also the* (same) *event of the beasts – one event befalls them: As one dies, so the other dies. Indeed, they all have one breath – <u>so that mankind has no advantage over the beasts</u>." For all is futile.* **20** *All are going to one place – all came from the dust and all return to the dust.* This is telling us that men themselves are beasts and that mankind has the breath of life just like the beasts do. When men die, they return to the dust of the earth just as all of the animals do.

Can you tell me what it was that mankind did or was doing that caused Ehyeh to regret that He had made mankind in the first place? Scripture tells us in **Genesis 6:5-6** that, **5** *"Ehyeh saw that the wickedness of man was* *great in the earth and that every imagination of the thoughts of his heart was only evil continually. 6 And it repented Ehyeh that He had created man on the earth, and it grieved Him at His heart."*

Scripture is not entirely explicit when it comes to explaining what it was that mankind was doing to corrupt themselves and the earth. However, the **Book of Yasher** and the **Book of Enoch** both tell us some of the answers to that very question.

The **Book of Yasher 4:16-18** says, **16** *"All of the sons of men departed from the ways of Ehyeh in those days as they multiplied upon the surface of the earth with sons and daughters, and they taught one another their evil practices and they continued sinning against Ehyeh.* **17** *And every man made unto himself an idol and they robbed and plundered every man his neighbor as well as his relatives and they corrupted the earth, and the earth was filled with violence.* **18** *And their judges and rulers went to the daughters of men and took their wives by force from their husbands according to their choice and the sons of men in those days took of the cattle* (livestock) *of the earth, the beasts of the field and the fouls of the air and <u>taught the mixture of animals of one species with the other</u>, in order therewith to provoke Ehyeh; and Ehyeh saw that the whole earth was corrupt, for all flesh had corrupted its ways upon the earth, all men and all animals."* The **Book of Enoch 7:10** says, *"They taught sorcery, incantation and the dividing of the roots and trees."*

Ehyeh told Noah in **Genesis 9:2** *"the fear of you and the dread of you shall be upon every beast of the earth and upon every bird of the air, upon all that moves upon the earth and upon all of the fishes of the sea"...* I believe that the reason Ehyeh told Noah this is that prior to the flood the animals were probably not afraid of mankind. This is

141

probably why mankind was able to make the animals interbreed with different species.

Ok, back to the subject: After the flood, Ehyeh made a renewed covenant with mankind and the animals. **Genesis Chapter 9** is where we find the information on this renewed covenant. Remember how I said that the renewed covenant probably has something to do with what we can and cannot eat. **Genesis 9:3** tells us that, "*<u>Every moving (swarming) thing that lives</u> shall be food for you; even as the green herb have I given you all things.*" If you will go back to the last paragraph on page 138 you will see that this is referring to the same thing. This is showing us that **Genesis 1:21** *and* **Genesis 9:3** are both referring to the <u>swarming</u> animals in the sea. <u>Some people say</u> that the swarming animals in the sea do not have the breath of life in them, so this verse is implying that we can eat the fish that are in the waters. However, Scripture tells us that we are not to eat <u>any flesh with the life (breath) in it</u>. The blood is what carries the oxygen (breath) to the bodies of both mankind and the beasts. When you catch a fish, it also bleeds. **Genesis 9:4-6** says, 4 "*But you shall not eat flesh with the life thereof, which is the blood thereof.*" – **This is the renewed covenant that Ehyeh made with all of mankind and all of the animals.** - 5 *And surely your blood of your lives will I require; at the hand of every beast will I require it and at the hand of man; at the hand of every man's brother will I require the life of man.* 6 *Whosoever sheds man's blood, by man shall his blood be shed: because He created mankind in the image of Ehyeh.*

Genesis 9:8-12 says, 8 "*Ehyeh spoke to Noah and his sons with him, saying,* 9 *and I, See, I establish my covenant with <u>you and with your descendents</u> after you;* 10 *And with every living creature that is with you, of <u>the birds</u>, of the <u>livestock</u> and of <u>every beast of the earth</u> with you; from <u>all that go out of the ark</u>, to every beast of the*

142

*earth. **11** And I will establish my covenant with you; neither shall all flesh be cut off any more by the waters of a flood; neither shall of there be a flood any more to destroy the earth. **12** Ehyeh said, this is the sign of the covenant which I make between me and you and every living creature that is with you, <u>for perpetual generations</u>":*

Notice if you will, that this does not mention the animals of the ocean. This is why many people believe that this covenant is not with the fish in the water.

The word "perpetual" is the same as "everlasting." This everlasting covenant that Ehyeh made with Noah and his sons and with the living creatures; the birds and the livestock and the beasts of the earth was originally supposed to be an everlasting or perpetual covenant for all generations. It was originally established from the beginning of time with Adam and Eve. Mankind was not supposed to eat the animals and the animals were not supposed to eat mankind.

We find in **Deuteronomy 12:23** that it says, *"only be sure that you do not eat the blood; for the blood is the life; and you may **not** eat the life with the flesh."*

Mathew 24:24 tells us to study to show ourselves approved. But it also tells us, *"the whole world would be deceived, <u>even if possible, the very elect</u>."* Here in America, we have all grown up with the inherited <u>tradition</u> of eating **meat** three times a day and this concept of not eating meat probably seems to be the most foreign thing you have ever heard of. I can tell you from my personal perspective that this is one of the most radical things I had ever heard of before. This was more radical to me than the 1st day of the week versus the 7th day of the week Sabbath. However, based upon the texts that I have written of thus far, I have concluded that the Scriptures do not condone the eating of animal flesh for food.

Let Me Count The Ways In Which We Have All Been Deceived

According to the way that the Scripture reads, it <u>appears</u> to be telling us that it is permissible for us to eat the fish from the waters. However, **Leviticus 17:14** adds a few more details. It says, "*... for it is the life of all flesh; the blood of it is for the life thereof, therefore I said unto the children of Yeshurun, <u>You shall eat the blood of no manner of flesh</u>; for the life of all flesh is the blood thereof, <u>whosoever eats it shall be cut off</u>.*"

This verse tells us that we are <u>to eat no manner of flesh</u> because whoever eats **any** kind of flesh <u>will be cut off</u>. This means that you need to be absolutely convinced in your own minds that those previous verses are in fact telling you that we can indeed eat the fish from out of the waters.

I realize that this everlasting covenant is a hard bit of information to swallow. I also know that the Scriptures tell us in **Leviticus Chapter 11** and **Deuteronomy Chapters 12 and 14** that we are to make a distinction between the clean and unclean animals. It says that we can eat any animal of the sea that has fins and scales. It also says that we can eat any animal that chews its cud and has split hooves. It also says that we can eat any bird that does not kill its prey. This was what I was taught at one time. However, Scripture also tells us to test all things.

Speaking of tests, have you ever heard of Daniel? Daniel was from the tribe of Yahuda. He was taken prisoner with a large group of young boys to Babylon when King Nebuchadnezzar destroyed Yerusalem. Daniel and three of his friends, Hananiah, Mishael and Azariah, were the only four boys mentioned by name. According to **Daniel Chapter 1**, Daniel and his three friends were placed under the supervision of Ashpenaz, who was the master of the king's eunuchs. **Daniel 1:5** tells us, "*The king appointed them a daily provision of the king's <u>meat and of the wine</u> which he drank*"...

But **Daniel 1:8** says, *"that Daniel purposed in his heart that he would not defile himself with the portion of the <u>king's meat, or with the wine</u> which he drank: therefore, Daniel requested of the prince of the eunuchs that he might not defile himself."*

Daniel 1:10-14 says, *"And the prince of the eunuchs said unto Daniel, I fear my master the king, who has appointed your <u>meat and your drink</u>: Why should he see your faces worse liking* (looking) *than the children which are of your sort? You shall make me endanger my head to the king. 11 Then Daniel said to Melzar, whom the prince of the eunuchs had set over Daniel, Hananiah, Mishael and Azariah, I beseech you, 12 <u>test</u> your servants for ten days; and let them give us <u>pulse</u>* (vegetables) <u>*to eat and water to drink*</u>*. 13 Then let our countenances be looked upon before you and the countenance of the children that eat from the portion of the king's meat: and deal with your servants as you see. 14 So Melzar consented to them in this matter and tested them for ten days."*

Daniel 1:15-19 goes on to say that **15** *"at the end of ten days their countenances appeared fairer and fatter in flesh than all of the other children which did eat the portion of the king's meat. 16 So Melzar took away the portion of their meat and the wine that they should drink; and gave them <u>pulse</u>. 17 As for these four children, Ehyeh gave them knowledge and skill in all learning and wisdom: and Daniel had understanding in all visions and dreams. 18 Now at the end of the days that the king had said he should bring them in, then the prince of the eunuchs brought them in before Nebuchadnezzar. 19 And the king communed with them; and among them all was found none like Daniel, Hananiah, Mishael and Azariah: therefore, they stood before the king."*

Daniel 1:20 says, *"And in all matters of wisdom and understanding, that the king enquired of them, he found* them <u>*ten times better*</u> *than all of the magicians and astrologers that were in all his realm."*

Daniel and his three friends had asked for pulse (vegetables) and water to eat instead of meat and wine. <u>(Pulse is a food that is sown, (planted)</u>. <u>It fits into the category of fruits and vegetables)</u>. As a result of Daniel and his three friends refusing to eat meat and drink wine, they were found to be ten times better (smarter) than the others when they were tested. Can you tell me the names of any of the other boys who were taken captive? No, you can't. That is because none of those other boys did anything that made them set-apart like Daniel, Hananiah, Mishael and Azariah did.

Daniel 1:21 goes on to say that *"Daniel continued even unto the first year of King Cyrus."* When you read the entire **Book of Daniel**, you discover that because of this one test of not eating meat or drinking wine, Ehyeh allowed Daniel to live long enough to become the chief adviser for at least 4 individual kings. Daniel was chief adviser to King Nebuchadnezzar, King Belshazzar, King Darius and King Cyrus.

This should be enough evidence for you to make up your mind that what I am telling you is true. However, I need to explain one other thing. I imagine that you have already thought of this. Didn't Simon Peter tell us in **Acts Chapter 10** that it is now okay for us to eat all of these animals?

The first thing that we need to remember is that Ehyeh does not change. The last thing that we need to remember is that Ehyeh does not change.

The first thing to understand about **Acts Chapter 10** is that this story is not about food. The food was a metaphor that was used as an allegory. This was the first

Let Me Count The Ways In Which We Have All Been Deceived

time that a person who was not from the tribe of Yahuda was accepted by Ehyeh into the family of Yeshurun.

According to **Acts Chapter 10**, *"there was a man who lived in Caesarea named Cornelius. Cornelius was a devout man who always prayed to Ehyeh. One day about the ninth hour when Cornelius was praying, a Malakim* (messenger) *from Ehyeh came to him and called to him by his name, Cornelius.*

The Malakim told Cornelius that Ehyeh had heard his prayers. He told Cornelius to send men to the city of Yoppa to get a man named Simon Peter. He said that Simon Peter would tell Cornelius what he would need to do.

When the Malakim had departed, Cornelius called for three of his servants and he sent them to get Peter from the tanner's home in Yoppa who was also named Simon.

The next day, while they were nearing the city of Yoppa, Peter who knew nothing of this, went up on the house top to pray at noon. Peter was hungry, and he would have eaten but he fell asleep and had a dream. In his dream, Peter saw a large sheet lowered down from heaven with all kinds of pictures of different kinds of animals portrayed on the sheet.

While Peter was still dreaming, he heard a voice saying, Peter, get up and <u>kill and eat</u>. But Peter answered back while he was still dreaming; Not so, Master; because I have never eaten anything that is common or unclean. And the voice spoke unto him again the second time, saying, what Ehyeh has cleansed, you shall not call common. This was done three times: and the vessel (sheet) *was received up into heaven again.*

When Peter had woken up, he doubted within himself what this vision which he had seen should mean.

At the same time the men who were sent from Cornelius' home asked if Peter was there. While Peter thought on the vision, the <u>set-apart mind-set</u> said unto him, behold, three men seek you."

Did you happen to notice that Peter told the voice that he had heard that he <u>would not kill and eat any of these animals</u>? And then when Peter had woken up, he was trying to make sense of what he had just dreamed.

Peter went down and met with the three men who had been sent to get him and the next day Peter and certain other brethren went to Yoppa with Peter and the three servants to meet Cornelius.

This is where this story gets interesting. When Peter and Cornelius had met, Peter said to them, "You know how it is an unlawful thing for a man who is a Yahudian to keep company with or come to someone from another nation; but Ehyeh has showed me that **it is now ok for us to kill and eat all types of animals**." **Whoa**, is that really what it said?

Let's read the end of this verse one more time. **Acts 10:28** says, "*...but Ehyeh has showed me <u>that I should not call any man common or unclean</u>.*" **Acts 10:34-35** continues on; 34 "*...Then Peter opened his mouth and said, of a truth I perceive that Ehyeh is no respecter of persons:* 35 *but he that fears Him and works righteousness in every nation, is accepted with /*(<u>by</u>) *Him."*

As I said before, this entire chapter is about Ehyeh accepting people from other nations and tribes and languages who are striving to become upright (Yeshurun) as Cornelius did. There was no indication that Peter ever ate any animals prior to this dream that he had or that he ever planned to eat them after the dream. It was simply an allegory.

Let Me Count The Ways In Which We Have All Been Deceived

I hope that this convinces you that Ehyeh does not condone the killing of his animals. Did it ever occur to you that the animals were actually created before mankind was created? The animals were all created on the 5th and 6th days, while mankind was the last to be created on the 6th day of the week.

If you are still not completely convinced, let's see what Yeshua had to say about the killing of the innocent animals. The following is an excerpt from **The Essene Gospel of Peace.**

"It was said to them of old time, 'Honor your heavenly father and your earthly mother and do their commandments, so that your days may be long upon the earth.' And next afterward was given this commandment, 'Thou shall not kill,' for life is given to all by Ehyeh and that which Ehyeh has given, let man not take away. For I tell you truly, from one mother (earth) proceeds all that lives upon the earth. Therefore, he who kills, kills his brother. And from him will the earthly Mother turn away and will pluck from him her quickening breasts. And he will be shunned by her Malakim, and Satan will have his dwelling in his body. **And the flesh of slain beasts in his body will become his own tomb. For I tell you truly, he who kills, kills himself and whosoever eats the flesh of slain beasts, eats of the body of death.** Because in his blood every drop of their blood turns to poison. In his breath their breath to stink, in his flesh their flesh to boils; in his bones their bones to chalk; in his bowels their bowels to decay; in his eyes their eyes to scales; in his ears their ears to waxy issue. And their death will become his death. For only in the service of your Heavenly Father are your debts of seven years forgiven in seven days. But Satan forgives you nothing and you must pay him for all. 'An Eye for an eye, tooth for tooth, hand for hand, foot for foot; burning for burning, wound for wound; life for life, death for death.' For the wages of sin is death. <u>Kill not, neither eat the flesh of your innocent prey</u>, lest you become the slaves of Satan. For that is the path of

Let Me Count The Ways In Which We Have All Been Deceived

sufferings and it leads unto death. But do the will of Ehyeh, so that his Malakim may serve you on the way of life. Obey, therefore, the words of Ehyeh: 'Behold, I have given you every herb bearing seed, which is upon the face of all of the earth and every tree, in which is the fruit of a tree yielding seed; to you it shall be for food. And to every beast of the earth and to every fowl of the air and to everything that creepeth upon the earth, wherein there is breath of life, I give every green herb for food. Also, the milk of everything that moveth and liveth upon earth shall be food for you; even as the green herb have I given unto them, so I give their milk unto you. **But flesh and the blood which quickens it, you shall not eat.** And, surely, your spurting blood will I require, your blood wherein is your soul; I will require all slain beasts and the souls of all slain men. For I Ehyeh your king is a strong and jealous king, visiting the iniquity of the fathers upon the children unto the third and fourth generation of them that hate me; and showing mercy unto thousands of them that love me and keep my commandments. Love Ehyeh your king with all your heart and with all your soul and with all your strength: This is the first and greatest commandment.' And the second is like unto it: 'Love your neighbor as yourself'. There is no other commandment greater than these." And after these words they all remained silent, save one, who called out: "What am I to do, Master, if I see a wild beast rend my brother in the forest? Shall I let my brother perish, or kill the wild beast? Shall not I thus transgress the law"?

"And Yeshua answered: It was said to them of old time: 'All of the beasts that move upon the earth and all of the fish of the sea and all of the fowl of the air are given into your power.' I tell you truly, of all creatures living upon the earth, Ehyeh created only mankind after His image. Wherefore beasts are for man and not man for beasts. Therefore, you do not transgress the law if you kill the wild beast to save your brother's life. Because I tell you truly, mankind is more than the beast. But he who kills the beast without a cause, though the beast attacks him not,

Let Me Count The Ways In Which We Have All Been Deceived

<u>through lust for slaughter, or for its flesh, or for its hide, or yet for its tusks, evil is the deed which he does</u>, for he is turned into a wild beast himself. Wherefore is his end also as the end of the wild beasts.

So always eat from the table (garden) of Ehyeh: <u>The fruits</u> of the trees, the <u>grain and grasses</u> of the field, <u>the milk</u> from the beasts and the <u>honey</u> from the bees. For everything beyond these is of Satan and leads by the way of sins and of diseases unto death. But the foods which you eat from the abundant table (garden) of Ehyeh gives strength and youth to your body and you will never see diseases for the table (garden) of Ehyeh fed Methuselah of old and I tell you truly, if you live even as he lived, then will the king of the living give you long life upon the earth also as was his."

The following verse is just one of several excerpts from **The Gospel of the Set-Apart Twelve** that tell us that we are not to kill or eat any animal flesh.

"Children are to be brought up in the ways of righteousness, <u>neither eating flesh</u>, or <u>drinking strong drink</u>; <u>nor hunting the creatures which Ehyeh has given into the hands of man to protect</u>."

As I said before, get your hands on all of these books and read them. You will see for yourselves exactly what the scribes and Pharisees have taken out of the Scriptures which you have at your home.

I almost forgot to share with you a couple of the most convincing verses I know of that convey the most dramatic expression of Ehyeh's disapproval of the killing of animals. **Isaiah 66:3** says, *"He that kills an ox is as if he slew a man; he that <u>sacrifices</u> (<u>slaughters</u>) <u>a lamb</u>, is as if he cut off a dog's neck; he that offers an oblation, is as if he offered swine's blood; he that burns incense, is as if he favors an* *idol. Yes, they have chosen their own ways and their soul delights in their abominations."*

But wait a minute. I thought that the Scriptures tell us over and over again that these are the things that Ehyeh wants from us?

The following verses should answer that question. **Isaiah 1:11-15** asks, **11** *"To what purpose is the multitude of your sacrifices* (slaughterings) *to me saith Ehyeh? I am full of the burnt offerings of rams and the fat of fed beasts: I do not delight in the blood of bullocks, or of lambs, or of the goats.* **12** *Who has required this at your hand when you come to appear before me to tread my courts?* **13** *Bring no more worthless oblations:* (Your) *incense is an abomination to me:* **14** *The new moons and Sabbaths, the calling of assemblies, I cannot* (deal with them anymore)*, away with them; it is iniquity, even **your** solemn meetings. My soul hates **your** new moons and **you're** appointed feasts: They are a nuisance to me; I am weary of bearing them.* **15** *When you spread forth your hands, I will hide my eyes from you: Yes,* (even) *when you make many prayers, I will not hear you: Because your hands are full of blood.*

Isaiah 24:5 says, *"the earth also is defiled under the inhabitants thereof, because they have transgressed the laws, changed the ordinance, <u>broken the everlasting covenant</u>."*

(Note): **Practically everyone has eaten animal flesh at one time or another. They may not have killed the animal themselves, but if they have eaten any of it, then they condone the murder of innocent animals. You cannot hardly go to any restaurant and order a salad without the cooks putting bacon bits or chicken bits on the salad. Many types of bread have L-cysteine added to the dough to make it** more pliable. Most of this L-cysteine is from human hair or chicken and duck feathers. Gelatin is also made from pig and beef tendons. When their bones are boiled, the water is drained and what remains is a gel-like substance. Gelatin is what marshmallows and most gel-type candies such as circus peanuts are made from.

If it has not already come to mind, answer this question for me. Did Ehyeh really institute the slaughtering of all of these animals and the killing of the Passover lamb every year at Passover? If killing and sacrificing animals for their blood is not what Ehyeh wants, then what exactly does Ehyeh want from his set-apart people?

- **Exodus19:5** says, *"Now therefore, if you will <u>obey my voice</u> indeed and keep my covenant, then you shall be a peculiar treasure unto me above all people: for all the earth is mine":*

- **Yeremiah 7:23** says, *"But this thing I commanded them, saying, <u>obey my voice</u> and I will be your Sovereign and you shall be my people"...*

- **Yeremiah 11:4** says, *"Which I commanded your fathers in the day that I brought them forth out of the land of Egypt, from the iron furnace, saying, <u>Obey my voice</u> and do them, according to all which I command you: so shall you be my people and I will be your Sovereign":*

Ehyeh does not want offerings and sacrifices (slaughterings) from any of the animals that He created. All He has ever asked for any of us to do was for us to obey His commandments and His ordinances.

15
What Are The (Real) Commandments of Ehyeh?

Many of you who have been reading this book have been associated with the "Christian" religion most of your lives. The reality of the fact is that if you had been raised in a Muslim community, you probably would have become a "Muslim." If you had been raised in a Buddhist community, you probably would have become a "Buddhist." That is just human nature. That is why Scripture says in **Revelation 18:4** for us to *"Come out of Babylon."* I have already gone over this earlier, but I also want to tell you that there are at least 74 other verses of Scripture which tell us in one way or another, that Ehyeh has called Yeshurun *"out of Egypt."* The word Babylon means, "to babble or be confused." One meaning for Egypt is "false worship."

Christianity has its original roots from the Yahudians (Judeans). The Messiah was from the tribe of Yahuda (Judah). The problem is that the Christian religions do not want to have anything to do with the Yahudians or their beliefs. This thought process is based on a major misunderstanding. Have you ever heard the saying, "You can't know where you are going if you do not know where you started from"? Scripture addresses this dilemma when it comes to the Yahudian (Jewish) religion. **Romans 3:1-2** asks and answers this specific question, saying, 1 *"What advantage then has the Yahudians?* **Verse 2** says, *Much in every way: chiefly, <u>because that unto them were committed the oracles of Ehyeh</u>."* The word "oracles" means, "wise counsel." In other words, it was because; that unto the Yahudians were committed the <u>wise counsel (words) directly from</u> Ehyeh.

Have you ever heard of the 613 laws of Yahuda (Judah)? I am sure you have heard of the **Ten Commandments**. Have you ever heard of living by faith? What was it that **Isaiah** said again? **Isaiah 24:5** says, *"The earth also is defiled under the inhabitants thereof, <u>they have transgressed the laws</u> and changed the ordinance, broken the everlasting covenant."*

Yahuda tradition teaches that there are 613 separate commandments (Mitzvot) or laws that mankind is supposed to follow and obey. The problem is that many of these laws do not apply to everyone equally. For instance, many of the laws apply to just the priests. If you are not a priest, then those laws do not apply to you. Many of the laws apply to women and their childbearing. If you are not a woman, then those laws do not apply to you. As you can clearly see, this long list is not universal for everyone, so they would not be from Ehyeh. This list of 613 laws is a man-made list of commandments that was compiled by a man named Rabi Rambam, who was considered to be one of the greatest scholars of all time.

Many people say that they "live by faith alone." **Hebrews 11:1** says, *"Now faith is the substance of things hoped for, the evidence of things not seen."* This scriptural definition is correct. A person cannot get anywhere in life if they do not believe in something or someone. However, **James 2:26** says, *"...faith without works is dead also."* So,

155

this would imply an action. This means that, "faith" is a belief and an action. Have you ever heard this expression before? "Faith is living by every word that Ehyeh says." That would mean that we are to do everything that Ehyeh commands us to do. We have to conclude that we cannot live by faith alone. We have to have action associated with our beliefs. Do not tell me what you believe; show me what you believe.

So far, we have come to the conclusion that the 613 commandments are not from Ehyeh, and we have also come to the conclusion that "living by faith alone" is not enough.

Now we get to go and look at the 10 Commandments. Let's find out if these 10 Commandments are actually the true commandments of Ehyeh? Would it surprise you at this point in this book to discover that they might not actually be the true instructions from Ehyeh?

These are the Ten Commandments that are found in Exodus Chapter 20 and in Deuteronomy Chapter 5.

1. *"I am Ehyeh your Sovereign, who brought you out of the land of Egypt, out of the house of bondage. You shall have no other gods before Me."*

2. *"You shall not make for yourself a carved image, or any likeness of anything that is in heaven above, or that is in the earth beneath, or that is in the water under the earth; you shall not bow down to them nor serve them. For I, Ehyeh your Sovereign, am a jealous Sovereign, visiting the iniquity of the fathers on the children to the third and fourth generations of those who hate Me, but showing mercy to thousands, to*

those who love Me and keep My Commandments."

3. "You shall not take the name of Ehyeh your Sovereign in vain, for Ehyeh will not hold him guiltless who takes His name in vain.

4. "Remember the Sabbath day, to keep it holy. Six days you shall labor and do all your work, but the seventh day is the Sabbath of Ehyeh your Sovereign. In it you shall do no work: you, nor your son, nor your daughter, nor your male servant, nor your female servant, nor your cattle, nor your stranger who is within your gates. For in six days Ehyeh made the heavens and the earth, the sea and all that is in them and rested the seventh day. Therefore, Ehyeh favored the Sabbath day and set it apart."

5. "Honor your father and your mother, that your days may be long upon the land which Ehyeh your Sovereign is giving you."

6. "You shall not murder."

7. "You shall not commit adultery."

8. "You shall not steal."

9. "You shall not bear false witness against your neighbor."

10. "You shall not covet your neighbor's house; you shall not covet your neighbor's wife, nor his male servant, nor his female servant, nor his ox, nor his donkey, nor anything that is your neighbor's."

As you know, Moses threw the tables of stone down onto the ground and broke them when he saw that his brother Aaron had melted the gold down and made the golden bull for the people to worship.

This is where it starts to get very interesting. **Exodus Chapter 34:1** says, *"And Ehyeh said unto Moses, Hew you two tables of stone like unto the first: and <u>I will write upon these tables the words that were in the first tables</u>, which you broke."* Take note if you will, that it says, "He will write upon these tables <u>the (**same**) words</u> that were in the first tables."

Below is a list of the Seven Commandments that are found in Exodus Chapter 34.

1. **34:12-16** says, **12** "Take heed to yourself, lest you make a covenant with the inhabitants of the land where you go to, lest it be for a snare in the midst of you: **13** But you shall destroy their altars, break their images and cut down their groves: **14** For you shall worship no other god: for Ehyeh, whose name is jealous, is a jealous Sovereign: **15** Lest you make a covenant with the inhabitants of the land and they go a whoring after their gods and do sacrifice (slaughterings) unto their gods and one call you and you eat of his sacrifice, (slaughterings); **16** And you take of their daughters unto your sons and their daughters go a whoring after their gods and make your sons go a whoring after their gods."

2. **17** "You shall make you no molten gods."

3. **18** "The feast of unleavened bread shall you keep. Seven days you shall eat unleavened bread, as I commanded you, in the time of the month Abib: for in the month Abib you came out from Egypt."

4. 21 "Six days you shall work, but on the seventh day you shall rest: in earing time and in harvest you shall rest."

5. 22 "And you shall observe the feast of weeks,

6. 22 –of the firstfruits of wheat harvest and the

7. 22 –*feast of ingathering at the year's end."*

Once again, the **1st Commandment** takes in all of **Exodus 34:12-16** which says, *"Take heed to yourself, lest you make a covenant with the inhabitants of the land whither you goest, lest it be for a snare in the midst of you: But you shall destroy their altars, break their images and cut down their groves: For you shall worship no other god: for Ehyeh, whose name is Jealous, is a jealous Sovereign: Lest you make a covenant with the inhabitants of the land and they go a whoring after their gods and do sacrifice,* (slaughterings) *unto their gods and one call you and you eat of his sacrifice,* (slaughterings). *And you take of their daughters unto your sons and their daughters go a whoring after their gods and make your sons go a whoring after their gods."*

Now compare the 1st Commandment in **Exodus 20:1-3** with the 1st Commandment in **Exodus 34:12-16**. Do you see the differences here?

Now let's look at the 2nd Commandment in **Exodus 34:17** and see if it lines up with **Exodus 20:4-6**. The 2nd Commandment in **Exodus 34** is, *"You shall make you no molten gods."* Now this time they both line up. Both of these are talking about not making idols.

The 3rd Commandment in **Exodus 20:7** tells us not to take the name of Ehyeh in vain; whereas the 3rd Commandment in **Exodus 34:18** says, *"The feast of unleavened bread shall you keep. Seven days you shall eat unleavened bread, as I commanded you, in the time of the month Abib: for in the month Abib you came out from Egypt."* Are you starting to see the issue here?

Let Me Count The Ways In Which We Have All Been Deceived

The 4th Commandment in both **Exodus 20:8-11** and **Exodus 34:21** are the same. Both of these are talking about remembering to keep the Sabbath day set-apart.

The 5th Commandment in **Exodus 20:12** is to *"Honor your mother and your father."* But the 5th Commandment in **Exodus 34:22** is, *"To observe the feast of weeks."* These two commandments have nothing at all in common.

The 6th Commandment in **Exodus 20:13** is, *"You shall not kill."* But the 6th Commandment in **Exodus 34:22** is, *"To observe the firstfruits of the wheat harvest."* Neither of these have anything at all in common either.

The 7th Commandment in **Exodus 20:14** is, *"You shall not commit adultery."* But the 7th Commandment in **Exodus 34:22** is, *"You shall observe the feast of ingathering at the end of harvest."* As you can clearly see, these two commandments have no similarities either.

At this point, we know that there are Ten Commandments in **Exodus Chapter 20,** but if you have been paying close attention you will see that there are only seven commandments in **Exodus 34**.

Didn't **Exodus 34:1** tell us that the second set of stone tables was supposed to have the <u>same</u> words written on them as the first set that Moses broke when he came down from the mountain?

Here is something else that is even stranger than that. Exodus 34:23 says, *"Three times in the year shall all your men children appear before Ehyeh the Sovereign of Yeshurun."* This verse says, *"three times a year."* But now let's count them out.

1. The <u>Feast of Unleavened Bread</u> shall you keep.
2. To observe the <u>Feast of Weeks</u>.
3. To keep the <u>Firstfruits of the Wheat Harvest</u>.
4. You shall observe the <u>Feast of Ingathering</u> at

the end of harvest.

As you can clearly see, this is saying that there are <u>four</u> feasts that we are instructed to keep and observe, not just <u>three</u>. Something is obviously amiss about this entire thing. Are there <u>Ten</u> Commandments, or are there just <u>seven</u> commandments? Are there <u>3</u> separate feasts per year or are there actually <u>four</u> separate feasts per year? Well, which is it?

With all of the scriptural violence that the scribes have done to manipulate and corrupt the Scriptures, would it surprise you to discover that <u>these are not even the actual feasts</u> that we are supposed to keep and observe?

16
The Cutting & Pasting Of The Scriptures

Scripture tells us that we are not to add to or take away anything from the Scriptures. So far, I have shown you several examples of the scribes doing this over and over again. However, now I want to show you several blatant examples of cutting and pasting that the scribes have done. If you have never seen this before, you will be shocked.

As I said at the beginning of this book, as much as the scribes have manipulated the Scriptures, Ehyeh has been able to maintain the integrity of his word despite all of their efforts.

Have you ever heard of the "**Documentary Hypothesis**"? According to this Documentary Hypothesis, the first five books of Scripture were morphed together by four distinctive groups of writers. This may be completely new to you, but I want to show you just one example that shows a blatant cut and paste being orchestrated by someone. We find this in **Genesis 26:34-35 and Genesis 27:46. Genesis 26:34-35** says, 34 *"And Esau was forty years old when he took to wife Yudith the daughter of Beeri the Hittite and Bashemath the daughter of Elon the Hittite:* 35

Let Me Count The Ways In Which We Have All Been Deceived

Which were a grief of mind unto Isaac and to Rebekah. – **Genesis 27:46** continues; *"And Rebekah said to Isaac, I am weary of my life because of the daughters of Heth: if Yacob take a wife of the daughters of Heth, such as these which are of the daughters of the land, what good shall my life do me"?*

Well, do you see it yet? Do you see the hyphen in the previous paragraph? This is the beginning of **Genesis 27:46**. That means that at some time or another someone cut and pasted all of **Chapter 27:1-45** into the place where the hyphen is. Get your Scriptures out and look at it for yourself. Please don't just take my word for it.

The following statement about the **Documentary Hypothesis** is taken word for word from **Wikipedia**. "The **Documentary Hypothesis** (DH), sometimes called the **Wellhausen hypothesis**, proposes that the Pentateuch (the first five books of the Scriptures) was derived from originally independent, parallel and complete narratives, which were subsequently combined into the current form by a series of redactors (scribes/editors). The number of these narratives is usually set at four, but the precise number is not an essential part of the hypothesis."

"The hypothesis was developed in the 18th and 19th centuries from the attempt to reconcile perceived inconsistencies in the biblical text. By the end of the 19th century it was generally agreed that there were four main sources, combined into their final form by a series of redactors, R. These four sources came to be known as the Yahwist, or Jahwist, **J** ("J" being the German equivalent of the English letter "Y"); the Elohist, **E**; the Deuteronomist, **D**, (the name comes from the **Book of Deuteronomy**, D's contribution to the Torah); and the Priestly Writer, **P**.

"The contribution of Julius Wellhausen, a Christian theologian and biblical scholar, was to order these sources chronologically as **JEDP**, giving them a coherent setting in a notional evolving religious history of Israel, which he saw as one of ever-increasing priestly power. Wellhausen's formulation was:

1. The Yahwist source, (**J**): was written in 950 BCE in the southern Kingdom of Judah.

2. The Elohist source, (**E**): was written in 850 BCE in the northern Kingdom of Israel.

3. The Deuteronomist source, (**D**): was written in 600 BCE in Jerusalem during a period of religious reform.

4. The Priestly source (**P**): was written in 500 BCE by Kohanim (Jewish priests) in exile in Babylon.

"While the hypothesis has been critiqued and challenged by other models, especially in the last part of the 20th century, its terminology and insights continue to provide the framework for modern theories on the composite nature and origins of the Torah and Bible compilation in general. The men who studied this hypothesis were considered to be renowned scriptural scholars."

Question: Have you ever heard of the **James Moffatt Translation Bible**? Mr. James Moffatt published his first translation version in 1922. Mr. Moffatt has published his version of Scripture with these JEDP writings being segregated by the different types of print fonts. It is my understanding that the (P) writings are in the normal font. The (J) writings are in italics. The (E) writings have a smaller font. And the (D) writings have the [ ] brackets around them.

The Yahwist or (J) writings are the oldest. They would be considered the original writings. Anything after that would be considered additional writings or the redacted writings.

The Priestly or (P) writings are considered to be the latest or newest writings. As it is stated, these writings came from the Priests during the time when they were in exile in Babylon.

According to the James Moffatt Translation, **Genesis 2:4** was originally the first verse of Scripture. And according to the Documentary Hypothesis, all of **Genesis 1 - 2:3** were from the (P) writings. It begins in the following way:

Genesis 2:4 says, *"These are the generations of the heavens and of the earth when they were created, in the day that Ehyeh the Sovereign made the earth and the heavens."* It continues on with, **Genesis 1:1** which says, *"In the beginning Ehyeh created the heaven and the earth."*

Another obvious cut and paste can be found in **Genesis 6:8,** which says, *"But Noah found favor in the eyes of Ehyeh. – And Ehyeh said unto Noah, come you and all your family into the ark; for you have I seen righteous before me in this generation."* At the place where the hyphen is inserted is where **Genesis 7:1** picks up. As I said before, get your own versions of Scripture out and check it out for yourself. You will be able to recognize that all of **Genesis 6:9-22** was probably inserted by the (E) writers.

Have you ever noticed that **Genesis 6:19–20** *and* **Genesis 7:9** both say for Noah to take two (2) of each animal on to the ark. But **Genesis 7:2–3** says that Noah was to take seven (7) of each animal on to the ark. What was the rule again? If there are two different versions of the same story, then one of them has to be inaccurate or altered.

One of the obvious examples of the cutting and pasting can be found in **Genesis Chapter 37**. Scripture tells

Let Me Count The Ways In Which We Have All Been Deceived

us that Yoseph's brothers sold him to the Ishmaelites. But then later on in the same chapter, it says that it was the Midianites who sold Yoseph to Potiphar. This entire story in **Genesis 37** is integrated with the E and P and J writings.

<u>The underlined words are from the (E) writings.</u> *The narrower italicized print is from the (P) writings.* The larger print is from the (J) writings. When you read these individual fonts independently of each other, you can see how the story changes.

<u>Genesis Chapter 37</u>

1 *And Yacob dwelt in the land wherein his father* (Isaac) *was a stranger, in the land of Canaan.*

2 <u>These are the generations of Yacob</u>. Yoseph, being seventeen years old, was feeding the flock with his brothers; and the lad was with the sons of Bilhah and with the sons of Zilpah, his father's wives: and Yoseph brought unto his father their evil report

3 *Now Yacob loved Yoseph more than all his children, because he was the son of his old age:* and he made Yoseph a coat of many colors.

4 *And when his brothers saw that their father loved him more than all his brothers, they hated him and would not speak peaceably unto him.*

5 And Yoseph dreamed a dream and he told it his brothers: and they hated him yet the more.

6 And he said unto them, hear, I pray to you, this dream which I have dreamed:

7 For, behold, we were binding sheaves in the field and, lo, my sheaf arose and also stood upright; and behold, your

166

sheaves stood around about and made obeisance to my sheaf.

8 And his brothers said to him, shall you indeed reign over us? Or shall you indeed have dominion over us? And they hated him yet the more for his dreams and for his words.

9 And Yoseph dreamed yet another dream and told it to his brothers and said, behold, I have dreamed a dream more; and behold, the sun and the moon and the eleven stars made obeisance to me.

10 And he told it to his father and to his brothers: and his father rebuked him and said unto him, what is this dream that you hast dreamed? Shall I and your mother and your brothers indeed come to bow down ourselves to you to the earth?

11 And his brothers envied him; but his father observed the saying.

12 And his brothers went to feed their father's flock in Shechem.

13 And Yacob said to Yoseph, Do your brothers not feed the flock in Shechem? Come and I will send you to them. And he said to him, here am I.

14 And he said to him, I pray to you, go, see whether it be well with your brothers and well with the flocks; and bring me word again. So he sent him out of the vale of Hebron, and he came to Shechem.

15 And a certain man found him and behold, he was wandering in the field: and the man asked him, saying, who do you seek?

16 And he said I seek my brothers: Tell me, I pray to you, where they feed their flocks.

Let Me Count The Ways In Which We Have All Been Deceived

17 And the man said, they have departed; hence, for I heard them say, let us go to Dothan. And Yoseph went after his brothers and found them in Dothan.

18 And when they saw him afar off, even before he came near unto them, they conspired against him to slay him.

19 And they said to one another, behold, this dreamer comes.

20 Come now therefore and let us kill him and cast him into some pit and we will say some evil beast has devoured him: and we shall see what will become of his dreams.

21 And Reuben heard it and he delivered him out of their hands; and said, let us not kill him.

22 And Reuben said to them, shed no blood, but cast him into this pit that is in the wilderness and put no hand upon him; so that he might free him out of their hands, to deliver him to his father again.

23 And it came to pass, when Yoseph was come to his brothers, that they stripped Yoseph out of his coat, his coat of many colors that was on him.

24 And they took him and cast him into a pit: and the pit was empty, there was no water in it.

25 And they sat down to eat bread: and they lifted up their eyes and looked and behold, a company of Ishmeelites came from Gilead with their camels bearing spices and balm and myrrh, going to carry it down to Egypt.

26 And Yahuda said unto his brothers, what profit is it if we slay our brother and conceal his blood?

27 Come and let us sell him to the Ishmeelites and let not our hand be upon him; for he is our brother and our flesh. And his brothers were content.

Let Me Count The Ways In Which We Have All Been Deceived

28 *Then there passed by Midianites merchantmen; and they drew and lifted up Yoseph out of the pit* and sold Yoseph to the Ishmeelites for twenty pieces of silver: and they brought Yoseph into Egypt.

29 *And Reuben returned to the pit; and behold, Yoseph was not in the pit; and he tore his clothes.*

30 *And he returned to his brothers and said, the child is not; and I, where shall I go?*

31 And they took Yoseph's coat and <u>killed a kid of the goats</u> and dipped the coat in the blood.

32 And they sent the coat of many colors and they brought it to their father; and said we have found this: know now whether it be your son's coat or not.

33 And he knew it and said it is my son's coat; an evil beast has devoured him; Yoseph is without doubt torn in pieces.

34 And Yacob tore his clothes and put sackcloth upon his loins and <u>mourned for his son many days</u>.

35 And all his sons and all his daughters rose up to comfort him; but he refused to be comforted; and he said, I will go down into the grave unto my son mourning. Thus his father wept for him.

36 *And the Midianites sold him in Egypt to Potiphar, an officer of Pharaoh's, the captain of the guard.*

There is one other thing that makes this particular story very unique. It said that they killed a goat and dipped Yoseph's coat in the blood. Then when the story was told to Yacob he mourned for Yoseph for many days. What is interesting is that according to the **Book of Yubilees**, all of this occurred on the tenth day of the seventh month. This is supposed to be the; Yahudians <u>Day of Atonement</u>. According to the Yahudians and the Messianic groups, this is the day when the e-scapegoat is to be released and

169

everyone is to afflict their souls by refraining from eating and drinking anything at all for the entire day and night. **Yubilees 34:19** actually says, *"And on this account it is ordained for the children of Yeshurun, that they shall mourn on the tenth of the seventh month, on the day when they brought the sad news concerning Yoseph to his father Yacob, that on it pardon should be sought by the death of a young goat, on the tenth of the seventh month, once a year, for their sins"...*

As you can now clearly see, this "Day of Atonement" is a man-made feast. It requires the death of a goat to atone for their sins. As a result, you can clearly see that this is not something that Ehyeh would require from his set-apart people. This Day of Atonement is just another false man-made feast day. This feast was not established until after Yoseph was sold into slavery.

Before I continue on, I want to say that you will have to look into this Documentary Hypothesis on your own. I just wanted to bring it to your attention. This was all new to me and I believe it may also be completely new to you as well.

17
North

The Messiah told us in **Matthew 7:15** to, *"Beware of false prophets, which come to you in sheep's clothing, but inwardly they are ravenging wolves."* This statement is pretty much self-explanatory. Most of us can see the apparent analogy. We have all seen the cartoons with the wolves sneaking up on their unsuspecting prey in sheep skins. It turns out that this Scripture verse has a far deeper meaning than what it appears to have. There is somewhat of a play on words here.

You rarely see wolves during the day time because they are nocturnal animals who generally hunt in the evening as it is getting dark. The following is a very good description of "The Wolf", as they know it over in the Palestine area of the world.

The wolf (Canis lupus) is found throughout the northern hemisphere, and it infests the hills and valleys of Palestine. The wolf is known everywhere as the foe of sheep, and it is the dread of all shepherds. The wolf is pictured as an emblem of ferocity and bloodthirstiness. Assyrian wolves are larger and lighter in color than those of Europe. Owing to the milder climate and the greater ease of obtaining food, they are not as gregarious as in

Let Me Count The Ways In Which We Have All Been Deceived

northern countries, but <u>they sally forth at night</u> to seize their prey.

There are two more verses of Scripture which speak in reference to wolves doing their hunting in the evening time. **Habakkuk 1:8** says, *"Their horses also are swifter than the leopards and are more fierce than the <u>evening wolves</u>"...* and **Zephaniah 3:3** says, *"Her princes within her are roaring lions; her judges are <u>evening wolves</u>"...* There is one final verse which refers to "The north and Assyria." **Zephaniah 2:13** says, *"And he will stretch out his hand against <u>the north</u> and destroy <u>Assyria</u>"...*

As you can see, I have underlined the words, "<u>evening wolves</u>, <u>Assyria</u> and <u>north</u>." Can you tell me what these word all have in common? Hopefully, I will be able to tie it all together so that you will understand this entire thing. Before we get too far into this, I want you to think about it for a moment and tell me when it is that the wolves make the most noise? Don't the wolves primarily make all of their howling noise during a full moon?

For those of you who know your Scriptures fairly well, you know that Ehyeh divided the twelve tribes into two separate kingdoms. **1 Kings 11:31** says, *"And he* (the prophet Ahiyah) *said to Yeroboam, you take ten pieces: For thus saith Ehyeh, the Sovereign of Yeshurun, behold, I will tear the kingdom out of the hand of Solomon and will give ten tribes to you."*

There was the Southern Kingdom, which was made up of the two tribes of Yahuda and of Benyamin. Their king was King Rehoboam, the son of Solomon. Their kingdom was established in and around Yerusalem. Then there was the Northern Kingdom. The Northern Kingdom was under the authority of King Yeroboam. They consisted of the other ten tribes who split away from King Rehoboam, son of Solomon, because he was too harsh and cruel. The ten-tribe nation of the Northern Kingdom all left Yerusalem and moved north to Samaria and they established their kingdom on the mountain of Ephraim.

Scripture tells us that this division of the twelve tribes was devised by Ehyeh. **1 Kings 11:33** says it was *"Because that they have forsaken me and have worshipped Ashtoreth the goddess of the Zidonians and Chemosh the god of the Moabites and Milcom the god of the children of Ammon and have not walked in my ways, to do that which is right in my eyes and to keep my statutes and my judgments, as his father David did."*

Yeroboam became afraid that his new-found kingdom of people would return back to Yerusalem to worship, so he had two calves/bulls made of gold. **1 Kings 12:29-32** says, **29** *"And he set the one in Bethel and the other put he in Dan.* **30** *And this thing became a sin: for the people went to worship before the one, even unto Dan.* **31** *And he made a house of high places and <u>made priests of the lowest of the people, which were not of the sons of Levi</u>.* **32** *And Yeroboam ordained a feast **in the eighth month**, on the **fifteenth day** of the month, like unto the feast that is in Yahuda and he offered upon the altar. So did he in Bethel, sacrificing unto the calves/bulls that he had made and he placed the priests of the high places in Bethel which he had made."*

According to this, Yeroboam chose men who did not know the instructions of Ehyeh to become the priests. Have you ever heard the phrase, "the blind leading the blind"?

Yeroboam was king over the ten tribes for 22 years. Over the next 241 years, eight separate monarchs reigned over these ten tribes. According to Scripture, none of them did right by Ehyeh. Every one of them did that which was evil before Ehyeh. King Hoshea was their final king.

Let Me Count The Ways In Which We Have All Been Deceived

2 Kings 18:9-11 tells us, 9 *"Shalmaneser king of Assyria came up against Samaria and besieged it in the seventh year of Hoshea.* **10** *At the end of three years they overtook it: Samaria was taken in the ninth year of Hoshea.* **11** *King Shalmanesar of Assyria did carry Yeshurun away to Assyria."*

For 241 years the Northern Kingdom was without any Levite priests. As a result, they were ignorant of the law of Ehyeh. They were proverbially in the dark. When they were taken captive by the Assyrians, they were carried away even further north. They were eventually assimilated into the other nations. Today there are not any people living with a true bloodline from any of these ten tribes. Have you ever heard the phrase; "The Lost Tribes of Israel"? That is exactly what it means. They have literally become lost. It was Ehyeh who allowed this to happen because they refused to return back to Him and His instructions.

By now you are probably thinking to yourself, why is he telling me all of this? As it turns out, according to e-Sword the word "**north**" is number H6828.

North - H6828

צָפוֹן צָפֹן

tsâphôn tsâphôn

From H6845; properly *hidden*, that is, dark; used only of the *north* as a quarter (*gloomy* and *unknown*): - north (-ern, side, -ward, wind). It also means, to hide or secretly reserve.

In other words, the word "North" is used to represent deception or ignorance. This will make more sense in the next chapter.

174

When Ehyeh chose Abraham, he said all families of the world would be favored through his descendents. As a result of these ten tribes being assimilated into the other nations of the world, each one of us may have a trace amount of Abraham's DNA in us.

It has been said that the Native Americans are from the lost tribes of Yeshurun. Is it any wonder that they chant the name, "Ehyeh, Ehyeh, Ehyeh" when they dance around the fire during their frequent ceremonial powwows?

18
The Battle Of Armageddon

Revelation 16:16 says, *"he gathered them together into a place called in the Hebrew tongue Armageddon."*

Practically everyone who has read the **Book of Revelation** has heard of the "Battle of Armageddon." Quite a few books have been written about it. A whole lot of sermons have been preached about it. Nearly the entire population of the universe is afraid of it. It has been compared to the war that ends all wars. It is supposed to be the final battle between good and evil, between Ehyeh the Sovereign and Satan, the adversary. All of the nations of the world are supposed to come together and battle in the valley of Megiddo over in Palestine in the last great battle at the very end of time. It is supposed to be the scariest thing in the world.

From the beginning of this book, it has been my intention to explain all of the intricate ins and outs of what I want to share with you about the Battle of Armageddon.

I am now going to use an allegory or parable that may or may not be very good. It is the only one I can think of at this time that will convey to you what I have to share with you.

As you know, an automobile has a lot of parts. It must have every one of its parts to function properly. It will not go if it does not have all of these parts: tires, battery, transmission, steering wheel, steering column, motor, drive line, axels, brakes, fuel tank, etc. It takes even more parts than that, but I hope that you get the point.

An automobile travels better on the "high-way" than it does on a dirt road. **Matthew 7:14** tells us, *"strait is the gate and narrow is the way which leadeth unto life and few there be that find it."* Have you ever wondered where the phrase, "Take the high road", might have come from? Where do you think the word "highway" came from? Remember what **Isaiah 55:9** said, *"For as the heavens are higher than the earth, so are my ways higher than your ways and my thoughts* (are higher) *than your thoughts."*

Ephesians 6:12 says, *"We wrestle not against flesh and blood, but against principalities, against powers, against the rulers of the darkness of this world, against spiritual wickedness in high places."*

From the beginning of this book, I have tried to show you that we have all been incorrectly taught when it comes to the telling of what time it is. We have been taught that the new day starts at 12 o'clock midnight or at sunset, when the Scriptures actually tell us that the day starts when the sun comes up. We have been taught that the day is 24 hours long, but then the Messiah himself said that the day is only 12 hours long. Ninety-nine percent of the people in America go to their assembly meetings on the first day of the week instead of the seventh day of the week as the Scriptures direct us to. That means that they do not even know when the week begins or ends.

Then we have all been taught that the months have anywhere from 28 to 31 days. Or if you grew up in the Yahudian religious faith, you start your months by watching for the first sliver of the moon to determine when the new month begins. As a result of this reckoning, the Yahudians have to add an additional 13th month every third year to make up for the time shortage.

The entire world has 365¼ days in a calendar year. And every four years we have what is called, "leap year." But when we begin searching for The Truth, we learn that there are actually additional Scriptures which were hidden from 99% of us which tell us that we are only supposed to have 364 days per year, every year.

We also discovered that every single day of the week got their names from false pagan deities. We learned that over half of the months have names that originate from even more false pagan deities.

We learned that every one of the set-apart days (holi-days) were established by man and were not established by Ehyeh. Then we find that the Scriptures tell us that we are to appear before Ehyeh three times per year, but then again is it actually four times a year?

We never did learn for sure when the true feast days were supposed to be observed, did we? Let's look into that right now. **Leviticus 23:6** says, *"On the fifteenth day of the same month is the feast of unleavened bread unto Ehyeh"*... and **Leviticus 23:34** says, *"Speak unto the children of Yeshurun, saying, the fifteenth day of this seventh month shall be the feast of tabernacles for seven days unto Ehyeh."*

We just learned in the previous chapter that Yeroboam established a feast on the fifteenth day of the eighth month so that it would be distinctively different than the feast that the people of Yahuda were observing in the seventh month.

So now then, can you think of what it is that all of these feasts have in common? Yes, they are all supposed to be observed on the 15th day of their respective months. Can you tell me what is so special about the 15th day of the month?

Do you remember when I asked you when it was that the wolves made the most noise? The wolves make the most noise in the evening on nights with a full moon. Wolves are nocturnal; they hunt for their prey at night. As I said before, the Pharisees have taught the people that the new day begins in the evening, and they also begin their new months when they see the first sliver of the new moon. Each moon cycle is 29 or 30 days in length, so the 15th day of each month will always be on the night of a full moon. This is exactly what Yeshua was warning us about in **Matthew 7:15** when he said, *"Beware of false prophets, which come to you in sheep's clothing, but inwardly they are ravenging wolves."*

Yubilees 6:23-38 tells us, "On the first day of the first month and on the first day of the fourth month and on the first day of the seventh month and on the first day of the tenth month (are) the days of remembrance and the days of the seasons in the four divisions of the year. These are written and ordained as a testimony forever. 24 Noah ordained them for himself as feasts **for (all) the generations forever**, so that they have become thereby a memorial unto him. 25 (because it was) on the first day of the first month that he (Noah) was bidden to make for himself an ark and on that (same day) the earth became dry and he opened (the ark) and saw the earth. 26 And (it was) on the first day of the fourth month (that) the mouths of the depths of the abyss beneath were closed. And (it was) on the first day of the seventh month (that) all of the mouths of the abysses of the earth were opened and the waters began to descend into them. 27 And (it was) on the first day of the tenth month (that) the tops of the mountains were seen, and Noah was glad. **28** And (it was) on this account that he ordained them (these days) for himself as feasts for a memorial forever and thus they are ordained. **29** They placed them on the heavenly tablets, (the constellations) each had thirteen weeks; from one to another (passed) their memorial, from the first to the second and from the second to the third and from the third to the fourth. **30** And all of the days of the commandment will be <u>fifty-two weeks of days</u> and (these will make) the entire year complete. Thus it is engraved and ordained on the heavenly tablets, (the constellations). **31** And there is no neglecting (this commandment) for a single year or from year to year. **32** And you command the children of Yeshurun that they shall observe the years according to this reckoning; <u>three hundred and sixty-four (364) days and (these) will constitute a complete year</u> and they will not disturb its time from its days and from its feasts; for everything will fall out in them according to their testimony and they will not leave out any day nor disturb any feasts. **33** But if they do neglect and do not observe them according to His commandment, then they will disturb all of their seasons and the years will become dislodged from this (order), [and they will disturb the seasons and the years will become dislodged] and they will neglect their ordinances (appointed times). **34** And all of the children of Yeshurun will forget and will not find the (correct) path of the years and (they) will forget the new months and the seasons and the Sabbaths and <u>they will go wrong</u> as to the order of the years. **35** Because I know, and I will declare it unto you and it is not of my own devising; For the book is written before me and on the heavenly tablets the division of days is ordained, lest they forget the feasts of the covenant and walk according to the feasts of the <u>heathen</u> after their error and after their ignorance. **36** <u>There will be those who will assuredly make observations of **the moon** – how it disturbs</u>

the seasons and comes in from year to year ten days too soon. (Ehyeh's true calendar has 364 days in a year, however, when you use the moon to calculate the months the year is 354 days long and so every three years it is necessary to add an extra month). **37** For this reason the years will come upon them when they will disturb (the order) and make an abominable (day) the day of testimony and an unclean day a feast day and they will confuse all of the days, the kodesh with the unclean and the unclean day with the kodesh; for they will go wrong as to the months and Sabbaths and feasts and yubilees. **38** For this reason I command and testify to you so that you may testify to them; for after your death your children will disturb them, so that they will not make the year only three hundred and sixty-four days and for this reason they will go wrong as to the new months and the seasons and the Sabbaths and the festivals and they will eat all kinds of blood with all kinds of flesh."

I realize that is a lot to take in, but did you notice all of the details in **verses 23 and 24**? It says,

1. The first day of the first month. This is actually the first day of **Spring**.
2. The first day of the fourth month. This is actually the first day of **Summer**.
3. The first day of the seventh month. This is actually the first day of **Fall**.
4. On the first day of the tenth month. This is actually the first day of **Winter**.

These **are** the **four individual stated days** of remembrance. They are the appointed days of the seasons in the four divisions of the year. These are written and ordained as a testimony forever. **Verse 24** said that Noah ordained them for himself as feasts **for (all) the generations**

181

forever, so that they have become thereby a memorial unto him.

So now let's look at that verse in **Revelation** that spoke of Armageddon. **Revelation 16:16** says, *"he gathered them together into a place called in the Hebrew tongue Armageddon."* This says that we need to look at the word Armageddon in the Hebrew language. Have you ever seen that before? Let's look at that.

The word "**Armageddon**" is actually a Greek word. E-Sword says it is number G717:

Armageddon - G717

Ἁρμαγεδδών

Armageddon

ar-mag-ed-dohn'

Of Hebrew origin [H2022] and [H4023]; *Armageddon* (or *Har-Megiddon*), a symbolical name: - Armageddon.

Armageddon is from two Hebrew words. The first word is "**har**". It is number H2022.

Har - H2022

הר

har

har

A shortened form of H2042; a *mountain* or *range* of hills, (sometimes used figuratively): - hill (country), mount (-ain).

As it says, figuratively speaking. This could be "top" or "head" or "chief." I personally believe that the word "har" is best translated into the words, "**Extremely Important**."

Let Me Count The Ways In Which We Have All Been Deceived

The second word is "**Megiddon**". Its number is H4023.

Megiddon - H4023

מגדו   מגדון

m^egiddôn megiddô

meg-id-done', meg-id-do'

From H1413; *rendezvous*; *Megiddon* or *Megiddo*, a place in Palestine: - Megiddo, Megiddon.

This says that is also from number H1413 which we have to look up.

Gad -H1413

גדד

gâdad

gaw-dad'

A primitive root (compare H1461); to *crowd*; also, to *gash* (as if by *pressing* into): - assemble (selves by troops), gather (selves together, self in troops), cut selves.

As you can see it is sometimes hard to convert Hebrew words into English. Several words can be used in English to convey the accurate meaning of the Hebrew word. But as I said before, it is the languages that were changed at the Tower of Babel. In addition to that, the scribes have intentionally manipulated the meaning of certain words.

As we just learned from **e-Sword**; the word "har" means, "**Extremely Important**." The next word is "Mageddon" which is "Gad" which means a rendezvous or assembly of troops. You generally have a rendezvous at a

183

specific set, appointed time. A feast day is also called a "**Moed**", accruing at a pre-set time. The word "moed" is also called a "congregation" of troops.

Well now then, have you put it together yet? The word "Armageddon" is the same as "**Mount of the Congregation.**" Have you ever heard of the Mount of the Congregation before? We find Ehyeh speaking to Lucifer here in **Isaiah 14:12-14**. He says, **12** *"How are thou fallen from heaven, O Lucifer, son of the morning! How are thou cut down to the ground, which did weaken the nations!* **13** *For thou has said in thine heart, I will ascend into heaven, I will exalt my throne above the stars of Ehyeh:* **14** *I will sit also upon <u>the mount of the congregation, in the sides of the north</u>":*

Have you put it together yet? This Lucifer (adversary) has said (in his heart) that he would exalt his throne above the stars of Ehyeh. The stars are for telling time by. He says he will sit also upon the "Har" (mountain) of the "Moed" (congregation, "Armageddon") in the sides of the "north", (darkness / ignorance).

This is telling us that this Lucifer will establish his own <u>false feast days</u>. By the use of deception, darkness or ignorance, he would establish his own false feasts. More people worship on the false feast days than on the correct feast days because they have all been deceived when it comes to times and seasons. The Battle of Armageddon is not a battle that will take place in the last days. The Battle of Armageddon is a battle that has been going on since the beginning of time. It is not going to be fought in any valley of Megiddo. It is a battle that is being fought in the mind.

Isaiah 55:9 said, *"For as the heavens are higher than the earth, so are my <u>ways</u> higher than your <u>ways</u> and my thoughts* (are higher) *than your thoughts."* Ehyeh's <u>ways</u> can be found in the stars. The constellations represent

184

Ehyeh's calendar that we are supposed to live by. **1 Thessalonians 5:1, 5** says, 1 *"But of the times* (signs) *and the seasons, brethren, you have no need that I write unto you. 5 You are all the children of light and the children of the day: we are not of the night, nor of darkness."*

In contrast **Isaiah 1:14** says, *"Your new moons and your appointed feasts my soul hates: they are a trouble unto me; I am weary to bear them."* Ehyeh has his stars, and the Pharisees have their moons. Ehyeh has the dividing of seasons, and the Pharisees have their full moons.

In conclusion, what do you suppose would be the purpose of anyone wanting us to be deceived when it comes to the times and seasons? Do you suppose that they want all of us to miss our appointed set times with Ehyeh? I personally believe that it is a must that we appear before Ehyeh on His correct **"Extremely Important Moeds"** (feast) days. If you do not know when those days are, you will be cut off.

19
Immanuel

We learned about the birth of the Messiah from the **Book of Matthew.** Yeshua's birth was actually prophesied a long time before he was actually born. We will begin here when a Malakim appears to Yoseph.

Matthew 1:20, 21 says, **20** *"But while he thought on these things, behold, the Malakim of Ehyeh appeared to him in a dream, saying, <u>Yoseph, you son of David</u>, fear not to take to thee Mary your wife: 21 She shall bring forth a son and you shall call his name <u>JESUS</u>: For he shall save his people from their sins. Now all this was done, so that it might be fulfilled <u>which was spoken of the Messiah by the prophet</u>, saying"...*

Since we are now looking at all of this with our eyes open wide, do you see any obviously erroneous statements here in these two verses? As we have already established, they would not have named him Jesus. Notice, if you will that this identifies Yoseph as the son of David. And finally, this says that this event had been prophesied by the prophet. For those of you who know your Scriptures pretty well, I am sure you know where we are going next, right?

1 Chronicles 17 is where we find the prophet Nathan telling King David that Ehyeh would raise up a son from

Let Me Count The Ways In Which We Have All Been Deceived

David's direct descendents, from whom He would build his family.

1 Chronicles 17:11-15 says, **11** *"It shall come to pass, when your* (David's) *days have expired that you must go to be with your fathers, that I will raise up your seed* (descendent) *after you, which shall be <u>from your sons</u>; and I will establish his kingdom.* **12** *He shall build me a house* (family) *and I will establish his throne forever.* **13** *I will be his father and he shall be my son: and I will not take my mercy away from him, as I took it from him* (Saul) *who was before you:* **14** *But I will settle him in my house and in my kingdom forever: and his throne shall be established for evermore.* **15** *According to all these words and according to all this vision, <u>so did Nathan speak to David</u>."*

Well, is that where you thought that we were going? There are two separate records of the linage of the Messiah in the Scriptures. Let's take a look at both of these genealogies. We find in **Matthew Chapter 1** that there are <u>28</u> generations from King David to Yeshua. We find in **Luke Chapter 3** that there are <u>43</u> generations from King David to Yeshua.

The lineage in the **Book of Matthew** has the lineage from David's son Solomon. Yeshua's father Yoseph was from Solomon's lineage. The lineage in the **Book of Luke** has the lineage from David's fourth son Nathan. Yeshua's mother, Mary was from Nathan's lineage. According to, "**The Gospel of the Birth of Mary**," Mary was from the family lineage of David just as Yoseph was. This means that Yeshua was from the descendent line of David through both his mother Mary and his father Yoseph. I had always been told that Mary was from the tribe of Levi. I wonder where that came from.

According to Yahudian law, the children are named after the lineage of the father. We have all been taught that Yoseph was not the actual father of Yeshua. That is what it implies anyhow. Notice if you will, what **Luke Chapter 3** has to say about the lineage of Yeshua. **Luke 3:23** says, *"And Yeshua himself, when he began to teach, was about thirty years of age, being the son* as *(was supposed) of Yoseph, the son of Heli"...* I have a question that we need to get an answer to. The question is, what does "as was supposed" actually mean?

Let's look and see what e-Sword says that it means. According to e-Sword, **"was supposed"** is number G3543.
was supposed - G3543

νομίζω

nomizō

It is from G3551, properly to *do* by *law* (*usage*), that is, to *accustom* (passively *be usual*); by extension to *deem* or *regard:* - suppose, think, be wont.

When the scribes wrote this passage with the words; "as was supposed" in parentheses, they did not change the meaning, but they did add doubt to the "customary legality" of Yeshua's birth.

According to the Prophet Nathan's prophecy, it was imperative that Yeshua actually be born from the seed of Yoseph. Yeshua had to be a direct descendent from King David's own lineage.

Now let's go back to **Matthew 1:22, 23** one more time. Let's read it as it is actually written this time. It says, **22** *"Now all this was done, so that it might be fulfilled which was spoken of the Messiah by the prophet, saying,* **23** *behold, a virgin shall be with child and shall bring forth a son and they shall call his name Immanuel, which being interpreted is, Ehyeh is with us."*

Can you tell me which prophet it was that actually made that statement? And more importantly, who the

Let Me Count The Ways In Which We Have All Been Deceived

virgin was who had the child and when all this actually did accrue?

Now at this time, we need to turn to **Isaiah Chapter 7**. You need to read almost all of **Chapters 7 & 8** to get the complete story, but I will do my best to make this a short explanation.

Approximately 748 years before Yeshua was born, the two kingdoms of Syria and Yeshurun joined into a confederacy to go against King Ahaz of Yahuda. When King Ahaz heard about their alliance, he and his people became very afraid.

At that time Ehyeh sent Isaiah <u>with his son Shearjashub</u> to meet Ahaz at the end of the conduit of the upper pool in the highway of the fuller's field. (Apparently it was a long trip). When Isaiah and his son Shearjashub met Ahaz, Isaiah told Ahaz not to worry about these two kings, because what they had planned would not come to fruition. Isaiah went on to tell Ahaz that within 65 years both of those kingdoms would fall. Historical records tell us that the kingdom of Yeshurun was taken captive to Assyria in 721 BCE.

Then Isaiah told Ahaz to ask Ehyeh for a sign which would prove that what he had said would come to pass. But Ahaz was too afraid to ask for a sign, so Isaiah told Ahaz what the sign would be. **Isaiah 7:14** is the optimal verse here; it says, *"Therefore Ehyeh himself shall give you a sign; Behold, a virgin shall conceive and bear a son and shall call his name Immanuel."*

We pick back up in **Isaiah 8:3** where it says, *"And I went unto the prophetess; and she conceived and bare a son. Then said Ehyeh to me, call his name Mahershalal-- hashbaz."* Are you seeing what was going on here? First of all, the prophet Isaiah already has one son whose name is Shearjashub. When Isaiah the prophet returns home from meeting with King Ahaz, <u>Isaiah</u> goes in to his wife the

Let Me Count The Ways In Which We Have All Been Deceived

prophetess and she becomes pregnant with another son. This means that she was not a virgin. They name the new baby boy Mahershalalhashbaz, but they actually call him Immanuel. It goes on to say that before the boy is old enough to say "mama" or "dada", the riches of Damascus and the spoils of Samaria would be taken away from these two kingdoms that were planning to attack the kingdom of Yahuda.

The name "Mahershalalhashbaz" actually means "swift to the prey." I am sure that you have heard the saying, "The hunter becomes the hunted." The kingdoms of Syria and Yeshurun were the attackers, but they quickly became the prey.

This means that <u>Ehyeh was with King Ahaz and the kingdom of Yahuda</u> all along. That is what the name, "Immanuel" means. It means, "**Ehyeh is with us**".

All of this took place about 748 years before Yeshua was actually born, so the name, "Immanuel" was not even intended for Yeshua.

What the scribes actually did was a masterpiece of cutting and pasting. The scribes cut the verse speaking of Isaiah's wife having a new baby boy and calling him Immanuel out of **Isaiah 7:14** *and* they moved it into the future prediction of Yeshua being born from a virgin.

We have established that Isaiah's wife was not a virgin because she already had at least one other son and we now know that this story does not even apply to the birth of Yeshua.

Something else to consider is what does that do to the idea that we have been taught about Yeshua being born from the Virgin Mary?

20
The Holy Spirit As Opposed To The Set-Apart Mind-Set

As you know, I do not like to use the word "holy" any more than I have to – mainly because, as we discovered earlier, that the word "holy" is from a pagan source. As I said before, I would rather use the term "**set-apart**."

We also went over the "renewing of the mind." This can only become possible with the support from Ehyeh.

Scripture tells us that Nicodemus came to Yeshua during the cover of darkness to ask him some questions. **John 3:3** tells us, *"that Yeshua answered and said to him, verily, verily, I say unto you, except a man be <u>born again</u>; he cannot see the kingdom of Ehyeh."*

John 3:4 says, *"Nicodemus said to him, how can a man be born when he is old? Can he enter the second time into his mother's womb and be born"?*

John 3:5 says, *"Yeshua answered, verily, verily, I say unto thee, except a man <u>is born from water and from the Spirit</u>, he cannot enter into the kingdom of Ehyeh."*

Let Me Count The Ways In Which We Have All Been Deceived

John 3:6, 7 says, *"That which is <u>born of the flesh</u> is flesh; and that which is born of the Spirit is spirit. Marvel not that I said to you, you must be <u>born again</u>."*

So then did you understand what Yeshua was telling Nicodemus? Every human is born from water. How many times have you heard some pregnant woman say, "My water has broken"? This is what it actually means to be "born of the flesh."

Since we cannot enter into our mother's womb again, the only way to be born again is to have a renewing of our minds.

The word "Spirit" is the "mind-set" of Ehyeh. We have to get this renewed "mind-set" from Ehyeh. Ehyeh is from above and we are below. In the previous four verses, it said that we must be born again two separate times. So then, what does it mean to be <u>born again</u>?

E-Sword says that the word "**Again**" is number <u>G509</u>.
Again - G509

ἄνωθεν

anōthen

an'-o-then

From <u>G507</u>; <u>from above</u>; by analogy *from the first*; by implication *anew:* - from above, again, from the beginning (very first), <u>the top</u>.

So being "<u>born again</u>" actually means to be "born from above" or to be "born from on high." It means that you receive the renewed set-apart mind-set from Ehyeh who is in heaven.

I have found eight separate verses of Scripture telling of the Spirit (mind-set) of Ehyeh coming down on eight separate people. The last one to be mentioned is Mary, the mother of Yeshua.

- **Numbers 24:2** says, "*and the spirit* (mind-set) *of Ehyeh came upon him* (Balaam")*.
- **1 Samuel 11:6** says, "*and the Spirit* (mind-set) *of Ehyeh came upon Saul"...*
- **1 Samuel 16:13** says, "*And the Spirit* (mind-set) *of Ehyeh came upon David"...*
- **2 Chronicles 15:1** says, "*And the Spirit* (mind-set) *of Ehyeh came upon Azariah the son of Oded":*
- **2 Chronicles 24:20** says, "*And the Spirit* (mind-set) *of Ehyeh came upon Zechariah"...*
- **Job 27:3** says, "*All the while my breath is in me and the spirit* (mind-set) *of Ehyeh is in my (Job's) nostrils."*
- **Matthew 3:16** says, "*And Yeshua, when he was baptized, went up straightway out of the water: and, lo, the heavens were opened unto him, and he saw the Spirit* (mind-set) *of Ehyeh descending like a dove and lighting upon him":*
- **Luke 1:35** says, "*And the Messenger answered and said to her, 'the set-apart spirit* (mind-set) *shall come upon you and the power of the Highest shall overshadow you: therefore, also that set-apart thing which shall be born from you shall be called the Son of Ehyeh."*

What I want to know is - did the set-apart mind-set of Ehyeh make the first seven men pregnant? Now I know that this sounds like a ridiculous question, but when you put it into perspective, did the set-apart mind-set in actuality make Mary pregnant"?

Read **Luke 1:35** one more time and you will see that it was the set-apart mind-set of Ehyeh which came upon Mary. This was so that Mary would be able to raise Yeshua up in the way that he should go. It was not until Yeshua was older when he met John at the Yordon River that the set-apart mind-set of Ehyeh actually descended upon him in **Matthew 3:16**.

Mary was never impregnated by Ehyeh as we have been erroneously taught. The scribes have intentionally led us to believe that false lie.

21
Adultery

Scripture tells us that adultery is a sin. Adultery is mentioned 40 times in 33 separate verses of Scripture. **Exodus 20:14** says, *"Thou shall not commit adultery."* This is considered by many to be the 7th **Commandment.**

The form of adultery that most people do not think of as adultery is to turn to another deity besides the Creator. Ehyeh hates adultery–especially this kind of adultery.

However, most of the times when adultery is mentioned, it is referring to a man sleeping with his neighbor's wife or when a woman is sleeping with a married man. These are the most obvious forms of adultery.

We have been learning about renewing our minds and I want to mention that those of us with a western mindset have no clue how the eastern mindset works. Here in America and many other places in the world, the mindset is that we can take anyone that we want home with us and there are not any consequences, provided we don't get caught.

However, we need to consider that the mindset was different with the Hebrew people. Since we have been learning about Yeshua, we need to look at the circumstances of his birth one more time. **Matthew 1:18** says, *"Now the birth of Yeshua the Messiah was on this wise: When as his mother*

Let Me Count The Ways In Which We Have All Been Deceived

Mary was <u>espoused</u> to Yoseph, <u>before they came together</u>, she was found with child of the set-apart mind-set."

The first thing that you must understand is that the word "**espoused**" does not mean what we have been led to believe. There was no such thing as "being engaged" to someone back in those days. The word "espoused" actually means, "to be married." So that means that Mary was already married to Yoseph. The next verse in **Matthew 1:19** confirms this when it says, *"Then Yoseph <u>her husband</u>"*...

Another thing about the Hebrew people is that it was the custom for the husband to go and build his new wife a new home before they consummated the wedding by sleeping together. Continuing on, **Matthew 1:19** says, *"Then Yoseph her husband being a just man and not willing to make her a public example, was minded to put her away privately."* The scribes have written this so that it implies that Yoseph was not responsible for Mary becoming pregnant. But what really happened was that Yoseph and Mary actually did get together, and they consummated the wedding before Yoseph left to build the new home for Mary. When Yoseph came back from building the new home to get Mary, he saw that she was already showing.

If you are willing to see it, you will understand that Yoseph was actually thinking on how he could privately put Mary away in order to cover up his own public embarrassment. Yoseph was not thinking of Mary's situation as much as he was worried about his own reputation. Yoseph was trying to think of a way to cover his own embarrassment.

I now have a question that I want you to ask yourself. Since Ehyeh hates adultery so much, do you believe that there is any way possible that Ehyeh would consider breaking his own laws by committing adultery with a married woman? Since Yoseph and Mary were already married, Ehyeh would never have caused her to conceive a child.

Let Me Count The Ways In Which We Have All Been Deceived

This is what the scribes and the Pharisees have been teaching us for thousands of years. We have all been taught that Yoseph was not the father of Yeshua. We have all been taught that Ehyeh hovered over Mary and she immaculately conceived. We have swallowed that entire lie, "hook, line and sinker."

Now that you have had your eyes opened so that you can see all of this from a completely new perspective, do you still believe the lie?

22
30 Pieces Of Silver

According to Scripture, Yeshua preached to the people for about three years. During that time, he continually contended with the priests because of their killing and slaughtering and eating of the innocent animals. The Levitical priesthood had to shut Yeshua up, because if the people started to believe what he was teaching, their entire way of life would vanish away, and they would have to find a new way of surviving. The entire tribe of Levites, including the women and children, survived off of the tithes and offerings from the other eleven tribes. Yeshua was apparently beginning to put a major dent in the Levitical priesthood's livelihood. They had to eliminate him.

The long and the short of it is that the Levitical priesthood had to somehow kill Yeshua with the authorization of the Roman government. That is why we read in **John 18:3** that Yahudas (Judas) came with an entire army garrison, along with members of the priests and high priests, to arrest Yeshua.

Matthew 26:14, 15 tells us: **14** *"Then one of the twelve, called Yahudas Iscariot, went to the chief priests and said to them,* **15** *what will you give me, and I will*

Let Me Count The Ways In Which We Have All Been Deceived

deliver him to you? And they paid him <u>thirty pieces of silver</u>." In this day and age, this would be about $30,000.

Can you tell me why Yahudas was paid such a high reward just for identifying Yeshua? Since Yeshua was the one who had been antagonizing them for three long years, why then was it necessary to pay someone that much money to identify someone they should have easily recognized? This is the $30,000 question.

Do you happen to recall that after Yeshua had risen from the grave, he entered into the upper room and all of the disciples were there except for Thomas? **John 20:19, 24-27** says, **19** *"Then the same day at evening, being the first day of the week, when the doors were shut where the disciples were assembled for fear of the Yahudians, came Yeshua and stood in their midst and saith to them, Peace be unto you ... __24__ But <u>Thomas</u>, one of the twelve, <u>called Didymus</u>, was not with them when Yeshua came. __25__ The other disciples therefore said unto him, we have seen the Master. But he said unto them, except I shall see in his hands the print of the nails and put my finger into the print of the nails and thrust my hand into his side, I will not believe. __26__ And after eight days again his disciples were within and Thomas was with them: then came Yeshua, the doors being shut and stood in their midst and said, Peace be unto you. __27__ Then he saith to Thomas, reach here with your finger and behold my hands; and reach here with your hand and thrust it into my side: and be not faithless, but believing."*

Thomas is called <u>Didymus</u> in 3 separate verses.

1. **John 11:16** says, *"Then said <u>Thomas, which is called Didymus</u>"...*

2. **John 20:24** says, *"But <u>Thomas, one of the twelve, called Didymus</u>"...*

199

3. And **John 21:2** *also says, "...<u>Thomas called Didymus</u>"...*

According to e-Sword, the word "**Thomas**" is number <u>G2381</u>:
Thomas - G2381

Θωμᾶς

Thomas

Of Chaldean origin (compare [<u>H8380</u>]); *<u>the twin</u>*; *Thomas*, a Christian: - Thomas.

This means that this was a characteristic of the man. He was a "**twin**". Let's look and find out what number H8380 actually means.
Twin - H8380

תאם תאום

tâ'ôm

taw-ome', taw-ome'

From <u>H8382</u>; *a twin* (in plural only), <u>literally or figuratively</u>: - twins.

Since Thomas was called Didymus, let's see what the word "Didymus" means. According to e-Sword the name, "**Didymus**" is number <u>G1324</u>.
Didymus - G1324

Δίδυμος

Didumos

did'-oo-mos

Prolonged from <u>G1364</u>; *double*, that is, *<u>a twin</u>*; *Didymus*, a Christian: - Didymus.

Let Me Count The Ways In Which We Have All Been Deceived

What we have learned here is that the Hebrew word "Thomas" actually means, "twin" and the Greek word "Didymus" also means, "twin."

This still does not tell us who this Thomas / Didymus is or what his true name was. It still does not tell us whose twin he was related to does it.

Have you ever heard of the **Gospel of Thomas**? It is another one of those unique books that we have not been told about. It is, however, one of those Scriptures listed at the back of this book. The **Gospel of Thomas** is relatively short, but for this discussion, the very first sentence in the book gives us a clue. It says, *"These are the hidden words that the living Yeshua spoke, and <u>Didymos Judas Thomas</u> wrote them down."*

Can we go as far as to conclude that this Thomas who was also called Didymos is the same man who wrote the **Book of Jude**?

The **Book of Jude** has only one chapter and we need to look at the first verse. **Jude 1:1** says, *"Jude, the servant of Yeshua the Messiah and <u>brother of James</u>, to them that are set-apart by Ehyeh the Father and preserved in Yeshua the Messiah and called":* Notice, if you will, that this says that Jude is the brother of James.

We now have all of the pieces, so we can start to put all of this together. Scripture tells us that Yeshua had several brothers. **Matthew 13:55** asks, *"Is not this the carpenter's son? Is not his mother called Mary and his brethren, <u>James</u> and Yoses and Simon and <u>Judas</u>"?* According to this verse, Yeshua had four brothers. Notice, if you will that one of them was named James and another one was Judas. Could this be the same Judas who wrote the **Book of Jude**? Could this be the same Thomas (twin) who doubted that Yeshua had been resurrected?

Could this be why Yahudas Iscariot had to be paid so much money to identify Yeshua? Is this the answer to the $30,000 question? Was it because Judas was actually the identical twin of Yeshua and only someone who knew both of these men such as Yahudas Iscariot could actually identify which one of these two men was actually Yeshua?

Is it possible that the scribes have taken all of the pertinent information out of the books so that we cannot completely substantiate this theory?

I personally believe there might be something to this hypothesis. If there is any truth to this supposition that Yeshua and Judas were born as identical twins, then that would lead us to the next vitally important question. That question is, - What does that do to the belief and understanding that Yeshua was the only begotten son of Ehyeh?

23
The Litmus Test

According to Scripture, Yeshua said, "Woe unto you, scribes and Pharisees, you hypocrites." He repeated this statement at least eight separate times. The scribes are the ones who wrote the Scriptures, and the Pharisees are the false preachers who are teaching the lies. **Yeremiah 8:8** tells us, "...*the pen of the scribes is in vain.*" **Yeremiah 16:19** also says that "...*the Gentiles shall come to you from the ends of the earth, and they shall say, surely our fathers have inherited lies, vanity and things wherein there is no profit.*"

As I have said before, the scribes have erroneously led the reader into believing one thing, when the intent is something that is completely opposite of what they have written. For example: What exactly is this telling us?

1 John 4:1-6 (KJV)
The Spirit of Ehyeh versus the Spirit of the Antichrist

[1] *"Beloved, believe not every spirit, but try the spirits whether they are of Ehyeh: because many false prophets are gone out into the world.* [2] *Hereby know ye the Spirit of Ehyeh: Every spirit that confesseth that Jesus Christ is come in the flesh is of Ehyeh:* [3] *And every spirit*

Let Me Count The Ways In Which We Have All Been Deceived

that confesseth not that Jesus Christ is come in the flesh is not of Ehyeh: and this is that spirit of antichrist, whereof ye have heard that it should come; and even now already is it in the world. [4] Ye are of Ehyeh, little children and have overcome them: because greater is He that is in you, than he that is in the world. [5] They are of the world: therefore, they speak of the world and the world heareth them. [6] We are of Ehyeh: he that knoweth Ehyeh heareth us, he that is not of Ehyeh heareth not us. Hereby know we the spirit of truth and the spirit of error."

The following is how this same verse should have been written.

1 John 4:1-6

[1] "Beloved, do not believe every spirit, but test them to see whether or not the spirits are from Ehyeh: because many false prophets (preachers) have gone out into the world. [2] This is how you will know the Spirit of Ehyeh: Every spirit that is from Ehyeh confesses (confirms) that Yeshua the Meshiach <u>came as a mortal human</u>: [3] <u>And every spirit that does not confess (confirm) that Yeshua the Meshiach came as a mortal human is not from Ehyeh</u>: This is that spirit, which is from the anti-messiah, which you have heard would come; (and) it is even now already in the world. [4] You little children are from Ehyeh and (you) have overcome them (false prophets, preachers) because greater is He (Ehyeh) who is in you, than they (the deceivers) who are in the world. [5] They (the false prophets, preachers) are of the world; therefore they speak of the world and the world listens to them. [6] We are from Ehyeh so those who know Ehyeh will listen to us; while those who are not from Ehyeh do not listen to us. This is how we will know the (difference between the) spirit of truth and the spirit of error."

Both of these two versions are actually telling us that

Yeshua came into this world as a human being. They are also both saying that it is the spirit of the Anti-Messiah if you believe Yeshua came into this world by any other means.

Those who believe Yeshua came into this world by Immaculate Conception have been deceived by the spirit of the Anti-Messiah.

24
The Switch

We have been learning that the scribes have corrupted and manipulated the Scriptures from the very start. We have also been learning that many of the things we have been taught about Yeshua were outright, blatant, fabricated lies. Many preachers teach that Yeshua came to fulfill the law. They teach that Yeshua is the fulfillment of the law. They teach that the New Testament has done away with the Old Testament laws. As a result of this teaching, many people do not read the Old Testament like they need to.

I previously showed you at the beginning of this book that the scribes like to use words in *italics* to manipulate and influence the direction of someone's thinking.

The scribes in the New Testament also like to quote verses from the Old Testament. There is just one thing wrong with this. The scribes like to change a few of the words in the quotes to make it read the way that the scribes want us to think. In a court room, that is called, "leading the witness."

I do not want you to take any of what I am saying for granted. I want you to get your own Scriptures out and have a look at the following verses and see for yourselves what the scribes have done to corrupt the following verses. Please read the following six verses of Scripture and tell me exactly what the "<u>it</u>" is specifically referring to.

Deuteronomy 30:10-15 says that 10 *"if you shall hearken to the voice of Ehyeh your Sovereign, <u>to keep his commandments and his statutes which are written in this book of the law</u> and if you turn unto Ehyeh your Sovereign with all your heart and with all your soul. 11 For this commandment which I command you this day, <u>it</u> is not hidden from you, neither is <u>it</u> far off. 12 <u>It</u> is not in heaven, so that you should say, who shall go up for us to heaven and bring <u>it</u> to us, so that we may hear <u>it</u> and do <u>it</u>? 13 Neither is <u>it</u> beyond the sea, so that you should say, who shall go over the sea for us and bring <u>it</u> to us, so that we may hear <u>it</u> and do <u>it</u>? 14 But the word is very near to you, in your mouth and in your heart, so that you may do <u>it</u>. 15 See, I have set before you this day, life and good and death and evil".*

As you can clearly see, the word "<u>it</u>" is used eleven separate times in the previous six verses. The "it" is referring to Ehyeh's commandments and his statues that are written in the book of the law.

At this time, I would like for you to turn to the **Book of Romans**. **Romans 10:1-3** says, **1** *"Brethren, my heart's desire and prayer to Ehyeh for Yeshurun, is that they might be saved. 2 For I bear them record that they have a zeal of Ehyeh, <u>but not according to knowledge</u>. 3 For they being ignorant of Ehyeh's righteousness and going about to <u>establish their own righteousness</u>, have not submitted themselves unto the righteousness of Ehyeh."*

In the following verse, we see that the scribes have changed three separate words. **Romans 10:4** says, *"For <u>Christ</u> is the <u>end</u> of the law for righteousness to every one that <u>believes</u>."* Let's see what this says when we go back to the original meaning of these three words: Christ, end, believes.

For **Christ** / "salvation" is the **end** / "purpose or goal" of the law, for righteousness, to everyone that **believes** / "obeys." Or, in other words: **Romans 10:4** should have said, *"For salvation is the purpose or goal of the law, for righteousness to everyone that obeys.* And once again, doesn't **James 2:20** say that *"faith without works is dead?"* Or is **Romans 10:4** trying to tell us that all that we have to do is believe in this Christ and we do not have to follow the law? All we really have to do is believe. Well which is it? Doesn't **Matthew 5:18** say, *"For verily I say to you, until heaven and earth pass, not one jot or one tittle shall pass from the law, until all is fulfilled."*

Romans 10:5 tells us, *"For Moses described the righteousness, which is of the law, so that the man who does those things shall live by them."* We must actually act on and do these instructions.

Romans 10:6-7 says, **6** *"But the righteousness, which is of faith speaks on this wise, say not in thine heart, who shall ascend into heaven? (That is, to bring Christ down from above:)* **7** *Or, Who shall descend into the deep? (that is, to bring up Christ again from the dead.")*

Question: If verses **6** & **7** are quotes from **Deuteronomy 30:12 & 13**, then what happened to the "it"? What happened to the commandments and the statutes and the law? Here again, the scribes have taken the commandments and the statutes and the laws out of these quotes and they have inserted Christ as a (anti) substitute to the law.

Ehyeh was speaking to the false priests in **Hosea 4:6** when he said, *"My people are destroyed for lack of knowledge: Because you* (priests) *have rejected knowledge, I will also reject you* (priests), *so that you shall no longer be* *priests to me: Seeing as you have forgotten the instructions of Ehyeh, I will also forget your children."*

Today's modern way of saying this same thing would be to say: Because you false priests have rejected the instructions of Ehyeh, I (Ehyeh) have rejected you so that you shall no longer be priests before me. Because you have rejected the knowledge of the law and have failed to teach my people, they will be destroyed because of lack of knowledge. Therefore, I will also reject your descendents.

25
Burnt Offerings And Sacrifices (Slaughterings)

If you were to ask someone where they would find the first time in the Scriptures where any indication of a sacrifice, (slaughtering) is mentioned, they would probably tell you that it is when Ehyeh made coats of skin to cover Adam and Eve's celestial bodies. They might even say that it was when Cain and Abel brought an offering to Ehyeh. They might also say that it was when Abraham cut all of the animals in half in **Genesis 15:9-17**.

Let's take a look at all of these three events for a moment.

1. Most people automatically assume that Ehyeh killed a couple of sheep to get the wool and cover Adam and Eve with the wool. However, if you will think about it for a moment, first of all, it does not tell us that Ehyeh actually killed any animals, let alone any sheep. Secondly, shepherds do not kill the sheep when they take their wool. They simply sheer the sheep. The sheep do not die during the sheering of the wool. Thirdly, it does not say that Ehyeh gave mankind any animals' skins. Ehyeh gave human skin to mankind to cover their celestial bodies.

2. When Cain and Abel brought their offerings, **Genesis 4:4** says, "*And Abel, he also brought of the firstlings of his flock and of the fat thereof*". Do you see where I have underlined the two uses of the word "of" in the previous verse? Take and change both of those of's, to the word "from" and see how it reads. It reads as follows: "*And Abel, he also brought from the firstlings of his flock and from the fat thereof*". Abel did not kill any of his sheep and bring veal and lamb chops to Ehyeh. What Abel actually did bring was milk and cream and cheese which was the produce from the sheep. Abel already knew and understood the commandment which said, "Thou shall not kill." Remember, this was the everlasting covenant. Abel would not have broken the everlasting covenant and killed one of Ehyeh's innocent animals and brought it as an offering.

3. Now let's look at that story about Abraham cutting all of the animals in half. Do you remember what I told you about the **Documentary Hypothesis**? Anytime that you read about a god telling anyone to kill any animals or to make a slaughtered sacrifice, you need to understand that this is coming from the priestly writings. Do you remember when Moses's wife had to circumcise Moses's son? This pagan deity was another god of blood. I am certain that Abraham would not have been considered an upright, righteous man if he had killed all of those animals. We need to understand that this story was inserted by the scribes.

Throughout the Scriptures, you will find the scribes and the Pharisees teaching that Ehyeh requires the blood of unblemished animals to atone for the sins of mankind. Go back through your Scriptures and count all of the animals that the Levite priests slaughtered so that they could have burnt offerings to send up to their false gods who required blood. Then, ask yourself what was it that they did with the rest of the animal that they did not burn on the altar? I will tell you what they did. They slaughtered them and fed their families with all of the remaining animal flesh that was left over. The Levites ate very well.

One animal per day was not enough. Every time that someone sinned, the people brought another innocent unblemished animal to the priests to be slaughtered and eaten by the priests and their family members. This went on day after day after day. This is supposedly because the blood of animals was not good enough to atone for the sins of mankind.

Eventually they <u>supposedly</u> had to kill Yeshua, the allegedly, only begotten son of Ehyeh, so that his so-called set-apart blood could atone for all of the sins of all of mankind.

We have all been taught that we need to be "washed in the blood." Question: Have you ever tried to wash blood out of your clothes before? Blood does not wash out once it has set in.

It is completely understandable how we have been deceived by the scribes and the false preachers. The following three verses are from **Revelation 22:14**. I have included all three of them as they are written in several different versions of Scripture. Pay close attention to the differences in the words, when you compare the **King James Version with the Revised Version** or the **American Standard Version**.

- **Revelation 22:14 (King James Version)** says, "*Favored are they <u>that do his commandments</u>, that they may have right to the tree of life and may enter in through the gates into the city.*"

- **Revelation 22:14 (Revised Version)** says, "*Favored are they that wash their robes, that they may have the right to come to the tree of life and may enter in by the gates into the city."*

- **Revelation 22:14 (American Standard Version)** also says, "*Favored are they that wash their robes, that they may have the right to come to the tree of life and may enter in by the gates into the city.*

As you can clearly see, the **King James Version** says, "Favored are they that do his commandments", while the **Revised Version** and the **American Standard Version** both says, "Favored are they that wash their robes."

Well then, which is it? Do we do the commandments, or do we wash our robes in the blood of the innocent slaughtered sacrifices. Let's see what Yeremiah has to say about all of this. **Yeremiah 7:22-24** says, **22** "*I spoke not unto your fathers, nor commanded them in the day that I brought them out of the land of Egypt, concerning burnt offerings or sacrifices, (slaughterings):* **23** *But this thing I did commanded them, saying, Obey my voice and I will be your Sovereign and you shall be my people: and walk you in all the ways that I have commanded you, that it may be well unto you.* **24 But they hearkened not, nor inclined their ear, but walked in the counsels and in the imagination of their evil heart and went backward and not forward.*"

Do you understand what you just read? Ehyeh said, *"I spoke not concerning burnt offerings and sacrifices, (slaughterings) to your forefathers. But I commanded them this thing, saying, obey my voice / my commandments and I will be your King and you will be my people. It may be well with you if you will walk in all the ways that I have commanded you."*

The Truth has always been here in the Scriptures if you take the time to look at all of this from the correct perspective.

26
The Word

I have been trying to show you how the scribes and the Pharisees have corrupted the Scriptures. They have tried to make us all believe that we do not have to follow the commandments. They have convinced the majority of us to believe that all we have to do is believe in the sacrificial atoning blood of this man called Jesus Christ who was supposedly immaculately conceived. The entire story of Jesus Christ hinges on the fact that he is supposed to be just as much of a god as he is a man.

The following verses are used by the majority of false preachers / Pharisees to drive the last nail of this entire deception into the proverbial casket. **John 1:1, 2** says, 1 *"In the beginning was the Word and the Word was with Ehyeh, and the Word was Ehyeh.* 2 *The same was in the beginning with Ehyeh."*

Do you remember what I said about words that have capital letters? Did you notice in the previous verse that, "Word" begins with capital letters? This means that in all probability, the scribes have in all reality, manipulated, or corrupted these verses in one way or another. Did you take note that the word "same" is also implying that it is the same as the "Word." Now pay close attention to these next

Let Me Count The Ways In Which We Have All Been Deceived

two verses and see how the "Word" changes to a "him." **John 1:3, 4** says, 3 *"all things were made by <u>him</u>; and without <u>him</u> was not any thing made that was made.* 4 *In <u>him</u> was life; and the life was the light of men."*

This is a very clever way of manipulating the Scriptures so that the majority of the people will believe that this is speaking of Yeshua. These four verses have whole heartedly deceived practically the entire "Christian" religion.

Have you ever heard of the **Book of Ecclesiasticus / Sirach**? This is another one of those books from the **Apocrypha** that was taken out of the **King James Version of Scripture**.

Sirach 1:1-9 says, *"All <u>wisdom</u> is from Ehyeh the Most High, and <u>wisdom</u> has always been with him, and it (<u>wisdom</u>) was before time began. <u>Wisdom</u> remains with Ehyeh forever.* 2 *Who has counted the sand of the sea, or the drops of rain, or the days of the world? Who has measured the height of heaven and the width of the earth and the depth of the oceans?* 3 *Who has searched out the <u>wisdom</u> of Ehyeh that goes ahead of all other things?* 4 *<u>Wisdom</u> was created before all other things and the understanding of prudence was before time began.* 5 *<u>The words of the Most High are the source of wisdom</u> and <u>wisdom's</u> ways are the everlasting commandments.* 6 *To whom has the root of <u>wisdom</u> been revealed and who has known <u>wisdom's</u> wise counsel?* 7 *To whom has the discipline of <u>wisdom</u> been revealed and made manifest (known)? And who has understood the multiplicity of her steps?* 8 *There is only one Most High Almighty Creator; He is the powerful king, who is greatly to be revered, who sits upon his throne and is Ehyeh the Most High of dominion.* 9 *He created <u>wisdom</u> in the Set-Apart mind-set and saw her and numbered her and measured her."*

The word "wisdom" is used twelve separate times in the preceding verses. Did you notice that it said in **verse 5** that "*The <u>words</u> of the Most High on high are the source of wisdom*"? If the scribes would have left all of this in the Scriptures, then none of **John Chapter 1** would have made sense.

If you will indulge me, I would like to write all of **John 1-4** with the word "wisdom" in the place of the words "Word" and "same" and the word "him" and see how it reads.

John 1:1-4 *says,* "In the beginning was <u>wisdom</u> and <u>wisdom</u> was with Ehyeh and <u>wisdom</u> was Ehyeh. <u>Wisdom</u> was in the beginning with Ehyeh. All things were made by <u>wisdom</u>; and without <u>wisdom</u> was not anything made that was made. In <u>wisdom</u> was life; and the life was the light of men."

As you can see, the "Word" in **John 1:1, 2** does not apply to Yeshua as we have been improperly taught. The same goes for the words "same" & "him" in **John 1:3 & 4**. From now on, mentally take these three (3) words out and insert the word "wisdom" in their place.

27
The Greatest Con The Christian World Has Ever Known

Trust but verify. I hope that I have shown you enough proof from the Scriptures themselves for you to realize that you and I have been deceived on practically every level when it comes to the differences between the false man who was called, "Jesus Christ" and the real man who was, "Yeshua the Messiah."

Please, do not misunderstand what I just said. I believe that Yeshua the Messiah actually existed in real life. But the man "Jesus Christ" only existed on paper.

In the previous pages, I have exposed some of the many misconceptions that have been perpetrated on the masses about both of these men. As I said at the beginning, The Truth will set you free, but first it will make you extremely upset. As another friend of mine likes to say to me, "Do not confuse me with the facts. I have already made up my mind."

For you to be willing to accept and learn any of what

Let Me Count The Ways In Which We Have All Been Deceived

I have shared with you, you must be willing to have a renewing of the mind.

We have learned that Yeshua did not answer to the Greek name of Jesus.

- We also learned that he taught that we are not to kill and eat any animal flesh.
- We also discovered that Yeshua was not all knowing and omniscient as we have been falsely taught.
- We learned that Yeshua did not say, "I am *he*" when he was arrested. What Yeshua actually did was to audibly speak the name of the father. Yeshua said, "Ehyeh."
- Yeshua himself said that there are only 12 hours in a day instead of 24 hours as we have always thought.
- We learned that Yeshua was never referred to as "Christ." They actually called him the Messias or Messiah which means deliver. He points us in the right direction. He did not save us by his atoning blood.
- If I haven't mentioned it before, Yeshua's apostles never did call him by the title of "Lord." It was either "Master" or "Rabi."
- We learned that scholars have determined that Yeshua was not born in the month of December, so the foundation of Christmas day is completely false.
- We have discovered that the scribes cut the story of Immanuel out of **Isaiah Chapters 7 and 8** and falsely inserted it into the story of the birth of the Messiah.

Let Me Count The Ways In Which We Have All Been Deceived

- We discovered that Yeshua's real father was Yoseph, from the line of Yahuda and that Ehyeh did not commit adultery with his mother Mary and make her pregnant.
- We have found that the reason that Yahudas Iscariot was paid such a high price to identify Yeshua is that Yeshua had a twin brother who was more than likely his identical twin.
- We have also determined that it is the spirit of antichrist to believe that Yeshua came into this world by any other means than through Yoseph and Mary.
- We have also learned that the scribes have intentionally subverted the Scriptures by putting "Jesus Christ" in the place of the law.
- We have learned that the blood of Messiah is not what it takes to enter into the new city. It is by obeying the commandments and statues and laws that Ehyeh commanded us to obey.

This is not by far the entire list of deceptions that can be found concerning Yeshua the Messiah in the Scriptures. There is more to search out and discover when you are looking at the Scriptures from the correct perspective.

I have shared with you, you must be willing to have a renewing of the mind.

We have learned that Yeshua did not answer to the Greek name of Jesus.

- We also learned that he taught that we are not to kill and eat any animal flesh.
- We also discovered that Yeshua was not all knowing and omniscient as we have been falsely taught.
- We learned that Yeshua did not say, "I am *he*" when he was arrested. What Yeshua actually did was to audibly speak the name of the father. Yeshua said, "Ehyeh."
- Yeshua himself said that there are only 12 hours in a day instead of 24 hours as we have always thought.
- We learned that Yeshua was never referred to as "Christ." They actually called him the Messias or Messiah which means deliver. He points us in the right direction. He did not save us by his atoning blood.
- If I haven't mentioned it before, Yeshua's apostles never did call him by the title of "Lord." It was either "Master" or "Rabi."
- We learned that scholars have determined that Yeshua was not born in the month of December, so the foundation of Christmas day is completely false.
- We have discovered that the scribes cut the story of Immanuel out of **Isaiah Chapters 7 and 8** and falsely inserted it into the story of the birth of the Messiah.

Let Me Count The Ways In Which We Have All Been Deceived

- We discovered that Yeshua's real father was Yoseph, from the line of Yahuda and that Ehyeh did not commit adultery with his mother Mary and make her pregnant.
- We have found that the reason that Yahudas Iscariot was paid such a high price to identify Yeshua is that Yeshua had a twin brother who was more than likely his identical twin.
- We have also determined that it is the spirit of antichrist to believe that Yeshua came into this world by any other means than through Yoseph and Mary.
- We have also learned that the scribes have intentionally subverted the Scriptures by putting "Jesus Christ" in the place of the law.
- We have learned that the blood of Messiah is not what it takes to enter into the new city. It is by obeying the commandments and statues and laws that Ehyeh commanded us to obey.

This is not by far the entire list of deceptions that can be found concerning Yeshua the Messiah in the Scriptures. There is more to search out and discover when you are looking at the Scriptures from the correct perspective.

Let Me Count The Ways In Which We Have All Been Deceived

28
The Pass-over Verses The Passover

We have just recently come into the knowledge of another piece of the puzzle. Just as I have already shown you, the scribes and Pharisees have misdirected everyone into looking at this next topic in a completely false perspective.

This new piece of information would not have made sense until we completely understood Ehyeh's 364-day calendar with the changing of the 4 separate seasons. There are 12 - 30-day months in each year. There are 3 months in each season. As you know, there are 4 separate days of remembrance which divide the 4 seasons. These 4 days stand alone. They are not a part of any month.

Before I explain this in further detail, I want to show you where I got this new thought from. **Genesis 32:16** says, Yacob instructed his servants to "pass over" the river. I read that verse and one thing led to another and I investigated to see how many times the words "pass over" was used in the scriptures and I discovered that they are used a total of 46 separate times. The definition of "pass over" is in essence the same thing as "crossing over".

Now that I have explained this to you, I want to talk about the "Passover". The scribes and the Pharisees have been instructing the people to observe the "Feast of Passover" on the 14th day of the month of Abib. It was during this time that the people were instructed to slaughter and eat the lamb.

However, we now know that Ehyeh does not want us to kill or eat any of His animals that He created. So now we must all look at this thing which is called "The Passover" from a completely different perspective. We now have the calendar in the heaven that we can look at. We now know that it is the "lamb" (Naphtali) that is the first constellation in the sky on the first month of the new year. It was during the month of Naphtali that the children of Yacob departed out of Egypt. This was the first month of spring which is where you get the "Abib" which means the "green ear".

Now that we have all of the components to this riddle together, we can put this puzzle together. As I said, this is not referring to killing and eating a real lamb.

As you know, the last day of the year is the 30th day of Zebulun. Then, the following day is when we have the "Day of Remembrance" which divides the winter and spring seasons. This is the "Passover" day. When we Pass over or cross over from the previous (old) year into the new year we are essentially conquering the lamb of Naphtali. The Passover day is the 1st day of the new year. And the following day is the 1st day of Naphtali.

Do you see how the scribes and Pharisees have completely deceived everyone into believing the lie about killing the lamb on the 14th day? Since the people use the false moon to determine when their new month begins, the 14th day of the month is always occurring during a full moon.

Now we can understand that statement about how an individual who is without knowledge is in ignorance. But once that individual has obtained the knowledge, the ignorance vanishes away.

29
Yeshua's True Birthday

We discovered in the previous chapter that the Passover is actually referring to the 1st day of the new year as opposed to the 14th day of the first month. Now that we know this new information, we can build on this and learn some new things about when Yeshua the Messiah was actually born. This is another riddle that we intend to solve.

It turns out that the Yahudian people have a tradition of putting a plate of unleavened bread and or a cup of wine out so that the prophet Elijah would be invited to come into their homes and be welcome for what is traditionally called the Passover Seder. Modern day Christians would not necessarily know of this because most of us have never heard of this Yahudian tradition. They get this from **Malachi 4:5** which says, *"I am sending you Eliyah the prophet before the coming of the great and awesome day of the Master"*.

So, what we know at this point is that it was at the time of Passover when Eliyah was supposed to come.

At this point we can go and learn what the Messiah had to say about Eliyah. **Matthew 11:13-14** says, "For all the prophets and the law prophesied until <u>John</u>. 14 And if you are willing to accept it, this is Elijah, who is to come". So, right here the Messiah was saying that John the Baptist was Eliyah. **Luke 1:17** tells us that he (John) shall go before him in the spirit and power of Eliyah ... to make ready a people prepared for the Messiah. **John 1:7** says, John came for a witness, to bear witness of the Light, that through him all *men* might believe.

Let's take a moment to review what we have learned so far.

1. Passover is actually on the 1st day of the year.
2. Elijah is supposed to come on the Passover day.
3. John the Baptist is Eliyah.
4. This tells us that John the Baptist was born on Passover – the 1st day of the year.

According to **Luke 1:35-36** the Malakim, Gabriel appeared before Mary when her cousin Elisabeth was already six months pregnant and told her that she was with child. This means that the Messiah would have been born six months after John was born. That would have been 180 days later which would mean that the Messiah was born on or near the last day of the month of Asher (The Upright).

Looking at Ehyeh's calendar, the Yahudians call this constellation Bethulah which is caller Virgo or the "Virgin". The word "Bethulah" begins with "Bet" which means "House". In Hebrew, the word "Bethulah also means "Bethlechem" which means "House of Bread".

What is unique about this particular constellation is that it is depicted as a virgin with a stalk of wheat in her hand. You make bread from the wheat.

So, what else do we know now?

Let Me Count The Ways In Which We Have All Been Deceived

5. The Messiah was born 180 days after John was born in the month of Asher.

6. This constellation was called "The Virgin".

7. It is also called Beth-lechem which means; "House of Bread". This is where the town of "Bethlehem" came from.

The day following after Yeshua would have been born would have been a day of remembrance; The feast of Tabernacles which stands alone and divides the summer season from the fall season.

John 1:14 says that; he (Yeshua) dwelt (Tabernacled) among us ...

So now we must ask ourselves if these pieces of the puzzle are enough to convince you that Yeshua was not born during the winter at Christmas time. You can also see where scribes and Pharisees got the original idea of the virgin birth from as well as why Yeshua was born in Bethlechem.

30
The False Pen Of The Scribes

As my friend likes to say; "Do not leave your brains at the door". It has been said that the pen is mightier than the sword. Authors and publishers write what they believe to be The Truth most of the time. However, all they really have to do is change a word here or there or insert a word where it should not be, or they may just add a few words and it changes the entire thought of the reader so that they can be mislead in the way that they should be thinking. I have already shown you several things that the false scribes have corrupted the scriptures but now I want to show you a few other examples of outright blatant deception.

First of all, we need to question our understanding of Ehyeh's true character. Does He make mistakes, and does He have to correct His mistakes? **Hebrews 8:7-8** certainly appears to indicate that Ehyeh made a mistake.

It says, **7** "For if that first <u>covenant</u> had been faultless, then should no place have been sought for the second. 8 For finding fault with <u>them</u>, he saith, Behold, the days come, saith Ehyeh, when I will make a <u>new covenant</u>

with the house (descendants) of Yeshurun (the Upright) and with the house (descendants) of Yahuda":

Notice if you will that the word "covenant" in **verse 7** is in italics. Once again, this means that the scribes have inserted this word into the sentence. What they have done is removed the word "people" from the sentence and substituted the word "covenant". If you will continue reading **verse 8** you will see that this will confirm what I am telling you. As you can see it says, "For finding fault with them". The "them" in this sentence is referring to the "people".

Malichi 3:6 tells us that Ehyeh does not change. When you continue reading **verse 8** you see that Ehyeh makes a "renewed covenant" with descendants of the upright people. There was no fault found with the covenant. Fault was found with the people so as they died off Ehyeh renewed His covenant with the next generation of descendants of upright people.

Another place where the scribes have manipulated the masses can be found in **Daniel 8:11**. It says, "Yea, he magnified himself even to the prince of the host, and by him the daily *sacrifice* was taken away, and the place of his sanctuary was cast down".

Notice if you will, that the word "sacrifice" is italicized here also. To understand this, you have to understand that Daniel got thrown into the lion's den in **Chapter 6** because he was caught praying to Ehyeh. King Darius was tricked by his rulers who were jealous of Daniel, and they convinced King Darius to implement a new law that said that no one could pray to any other god or person for thirty days or that person would be thrown into the lion's den. Daniel prayed three times a day just like King David did. The people prayed to Ehyeh in the morning and at noon, and in the evening.

Let Me Count The Ways In Which We Have All Been Deceived

It is our belief that the word "sacrifice" was inserted in this verse to take the place of the word "prayer". It was the "daily prayer" that was taken away.

Luke Chapter 1 tells us that Zaccharias was praying to Ehyeh for a child for himself and his wife during the morning prayer when the Malakim Gabriel came to answer his prayer. **Verse 10** says, And the whole multitude of the people were praying outside at the time of incense. (At the time of prayer). **Verse 13** says, "But the Malakim said unto him, Fear not, Zacharias: for your prayer is heard; and your wife Elisabeth shall bear you a son, and you shall call his name John".

Acts 10:9 says, "On the morrow, as they went on their journey, and drew nigh unto the city, Peter went up upon the housetop to pray about the sixth hour". This was the noon time prayer.

Acts 3:1 says, "Now Peter and John went up together into the temple at the hour of prayer, *being* the ninth hour". This would have been during the evening prayer.

Jeremiah 31:35 says, Thus, saith Ehyeh, which gives the sun for a light by day"...

Using these verses of Scripture, we can first of all conclude that the days begin when the sun comes up in the mornings. You need to understand that back in those days the people did not keep track of time by a clock on the wall or a watch on their wrists. What they did was, they stepped outside and judged what time of the day it was by the position of the sun. Morning would have been the first hour. Noon would have been the sixth hour. And early evening would have been the ninth hour. As you can see from these verses of scripture there were three separate times of prayer. First there was morning prayer when the sun came up. Then there was the sixth hour of prayer which would have been at or near noon. Then there would have been the ninth hour of prayer which would have been in the evening.

You may be thinking to yourselves, "What difference does it make when we pray"? Well, first of all, there are several individual verses of scripture that we need to consider.

Hosea 4:6 say, "My people are destroyed for lack of knowledge".

Psalms 69:13 says, "But as for me, my prayer *is* unto You, O Ehyeh, *in* an acceptable time":

Proverbs 15:8 says, "The sacrifice (prayer) of the wicked *is* an abomination to Ehyeh: but the prayer of the upright *is* His delight".

Proverbs 28:9 says, "He that turns away his ear from hearing the instructions, even his prayer *shall be* an abomination".

Matthew 24:15 speaks of the abomination of desolation, spoken of by Daniel the prophet.

It is the "daily prayer" that has been taken away, which is the abomination of desolation spoken of by Daniel the prophet.

We have all been taught that we can pray to Ehyeh at any time of the day and expect Ehyeh to answer our prayers. I am sure that He hears all of our prayers, but He may not be answering them when we do not petition Him or pray to him at the correct times of the day.

The majority of us have never been taught any of this. Now you have an idea what it means when it says, "The pen of the scribes is in vain".

31
They Have Changed The Ordinance

Isaiah 24:5 says, *"The earth is defiled under the inhabitants thereof, because they have transgressed the laws, changed the ordinance, broken the everlasting covenant."* We have already gone over how all the people have transgressed the laws. We have also learned what it means when it says that they have broken the everlasting covenant. Now we need to understand what it means when it says that they have "changed the ordinance."

According to e-Sword the word "**ordinance**" is number H2706.

Ordinance - H2706

חק

chôq

khoke

From H2710; an *enactment*, hence an *appointment* (of time, space, quantity, labor or usage): - appointed, bound, commandment, convenient, custom, decree (-d), due, law, measure, X necessary, ordinance (-nary), portion, <u>set time</u>, statute, task.

In other words, an "ordinance" is an established, appointed, set time. For instance, if you are to be at court at a preset time and you are late, then you can be held in contempt. The same could be said if you are supposed to be somewhere to see your daughter or son getting married and you show up on the wrong day.

This verse in **Isaiah 24:5** clearly indicates that changing the ordinance is a very bad thing to do. It was Ehyeh, the Creator of the entire cosmos, who established these ordinances from the beginning of time. It is mankind who has altered these established dates.

Job 1:6 tells us, "*There was <u>a day</u> when the sons of Ehyeh came to present themselves before the Sovereign*"... **Job 2:1** also says, "*Again there was <u>a day</u> when the sons of Ehyeh came to present themselves before the Sovereign*"... Can you tell me what day it was that the sons of Ehyeh showed up? We can get a hint from this next verse of Scripture.

Yeremiah 31:35 says, "*Thus saith Ehyeh, which gave the sun for a light by day and <u>the ordinances of the moon</u> and of the stars for a light by night*".

We have already gone over the "sun for a light by day", meaning that a day does not start until the sun comes up. We also went over "the stars for a light by night", meaning that the stars are for determining the months of the year. However, we have not yet discussed "the ordinances of the moon."

Exodus 23:14 says, "*Three times thou shalt keep a feast unto me in the year.*" **Exodus 23:17** says, "*Three times in the year all thy males shall appear before Ehyeh your

Sovereign." **Deuteronomy 16:16** also says, *"Three times in a year shall all thy males appear before Ehyeh your* Sovereign *in the place which he shall choose; in* <u>the feast of unleavened bread</u> *and in* <u>the feast of weeks</u> *and in* <u>the feast of tabernacles</u>*".*

According to the Scriptures which we have access to, the three times that we are told that we are supposed to appear before Ehyeh are the Feast of Unleavened Bread, the Feast of Weeks / Pentecost and the Feast of Tabernacles. Let's turn to **Leviticus Chapter 23** and see exactly what it says about these three feasts.

1. **Leviticus 23:6** says, *"And <u>on the fifteenth day</u> of the same* (first) *month is <u>the feast of unleavened bread</u> unto Ehyeh: Seven days you must eat unleavened bread."*

2. **Leviticus 23:16** says, *"Even unto the morrow after the seventh Sabbath shall you number fifty days".* This fifty-day count also lands <u>on the fifteenth day</u> of the third month, (this is <u>the feast of weeks or Pentecost</u>).

3. **Leviticus 23:34** says, *"Speak unto the children of Yeshurun, saying, <u>the fifteenth day</u> of this seventh month shall be <u>the feast of tabernacles</u>".*

As you can clearly see, all three of these feasts are on the <u>fifteenth day</u> of the month. Can you think of anything familiar about this that you read about previously in **Chapter 17** which was titled, **"North"**?

Do you remember what I told you about Yeroboam changing the feast day to the <u>fifteenth day</u> of the eighth month back on <u>page 173</u>? When the people are using the new moon to determine the beginning of the month, the

233

fifteenth day is always exactly in the middle of the month. Consequently, the moon is always, always in the full moon stage on the fifteenth night of the month. As a result of this evidence, we must once again conclude that these are not the correct ordinances of the moon.

Do you recall how I showed you back on <u>pages 80 & 81</u> that the scribes have caused the words moon and month to be used interchangeably. This should actually be "**the ordinances of the months**."

Back on <u>page 180</u> I showed you that there are actually four times per year when we are supposed to appear before Ehyeh. Once again, they are the:

1. The day before the first day of the month, which is the first day of **Spring**.

2. The day before the first day of the fourth month, which is the first day of **Summer**.

3. The day before the first day of the seventh month, which is the first day of **Fall**.

4. The day before the first day of the tenth month, which is the first day of **Winter**.

<u>New – Additional Information</u>

It turns out that these four days always land on the third (3rd) day (Tuesday) of the week, every 91 days from each other. – **<u>September 6, 2022 is the first day of Fall.</u>**

Daniel was thrown into the lions den because he refused to stop praying **<u>three (3) times a day</u>**. **We are supposed to appear before Ehyeh 3 times a day, (morning, noon, and evening).**

32
Ehyeh's 364-Day Calendar

1 **Thessalonians 5:1, 4, 5** says, 1 *"Concerning the times and the seasons, brethren ...* **4** *you are not in darkness ... you are all the children of light and the children of the day* (wisdom): **5** *we are not of the night, nor of darkness* (ignorance)."

Scripture tells us in **Genesis 1:19** that Ehyeh put the sun and the stars in the heavens on the fourth day of the seven-day creation week. This means that the first day of the year will always be on the third day of the week (Tuesday) of spring. This is the first (1st) feast day of the year that we are supposed to appear before Ehyeh.

Three days later Ehyeh rested on the seventh day Sabbath day which is the perpetual day of rest which we observe every seventh day. The Sabbath is the (weekly) feast day that we are commanded to guard and observe.

Then there are three months with thirty days per month and after that you have the first day of summer. When this day is added to the three months with thirty days per month, you get ninety-one days per season. Ninety-one days divides into thirteen complete, seven-day weeks. Thirteen weeks per season times four seasons makes it exactly 52 weeks per year.

The first third day (Tuesday) is always going to be the first day of summer. This is the second (2nd) feast day of the year when we are supposed to appear before Ehyeh. Then there are three more months with thirty days per month, followed by the first day of fall.

The first third day of the week is always going to be the first day of fall. This is the third (3rd) feast day of the year when we are supposed to appear before Ehyeh. Then there are three more months with thirty days per month and we have the first day of winter.

The first third day (Tuesday) is always going to be the first day of winter. This is the fourth (4th) feast day of the year when we are supposed to appear before Ehyeh. Then comes three more months with thirty days per month and after that we have the first day of spring.

Each season has 91 days per season. There are four seasons, so when you multiply 91 days times four seasons, you will always come up with a complete year of 364 days.

We have been deceived on practically every level when it comes to understanding how to determine what time it is.

We have been falsely taught that:

1. The new day begins at midnight or sunset instead of at sunrise as Scripture says.
2. The new week begins on Monday instead of Sunday.
3. The seventh day Sabbath is on Sunday instead of Saturday.

4. The New Year begins in the winter instead of at the beginning of the spring season.

5. There are 365¼ days in a year instead of the true 364-day year.

6. There are only three feasts per year instead of four.

7. The moon is the lesser light instead of the stars.

8. We are to observe the appointed feast days on the fifteenth day of the month instead of the first day of each month.

9. We are supposed to start the months by using the sighting of the new moon.

10. There is supposed to be a thirteenth month every third year.

11. We are supposed to observe the Sabbath for an entire 24 hours instead of just 12 hours of daylight.

12. The stars / constellations do not have anything to do with determining true time.

13. The months can have between 28 and 31 days instead of the 30 days per month.

14. We were also erroneously taught that we were supposed to use the equinoxes and the solstices to determine our seasons. However these are based upon the rotation of the earth on its axes and not the stars.

We were never taught that:

14. Many of the names of the months that we use originated from the names of false pagan deities.

15. The days of the week that we use were named after even more false pagan deities.

16. The names of the months of the year were connected with the sons of Yacob.

I cannot stress to you enough that we must align ourselves up with Ehyeh and his original calendar and observe his four seasonal Moeds, (set appointed feasts) which the Sovereign Ehyeh ordained and established in the very first year of creation. All other feast days are the invention of man and are from the imagination of mankind. By observing any other feast day, you are following after vain things. **Psalms 19:11** says, *"Moreover by* (doing/observing) *them is thy servant warned: and in the keeping of these* (ordinances) *there is great reward."*

Without exception, the first day of each season, including the New Year, will always begin on the third day of the week, (Tuesday) every time.

1 Thessalonians 5:1, 5 says, 1 *"But of the times and the seasons, brethren ... 5 Ye are all the children of light, and the children of the day: we are not of the night, nor of darkness,* (ignorance)."

Let Me Count The Ways In Which We Have All Been Deceived

Ehyeh's 364-Day Calendar Year

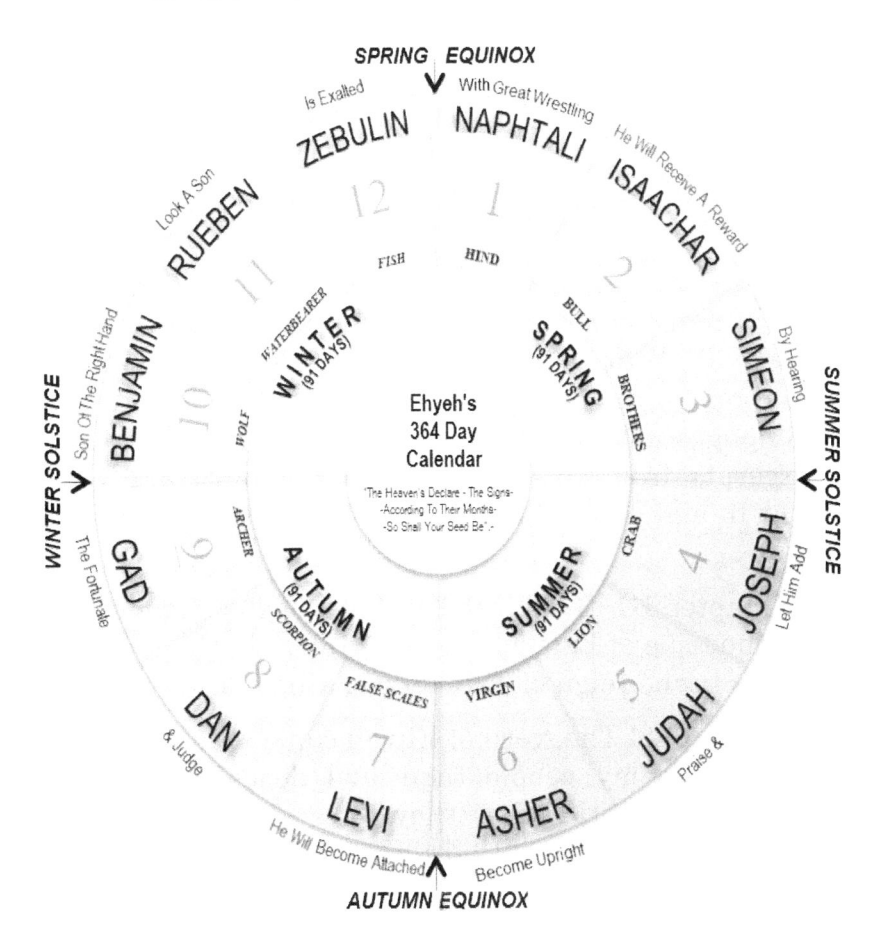

Let Me Count The Ways In Which We Have All Been Deceived

33
2 Esdras

Of all of the Scriptural books that I have personally read, I have found that the **2ⁿᵈ Book of Esdras** has some of the most profound explanations of many of Ehyeh's instructions. This book is only 33 pages long and it has 16 chapters. I have taken a few excerpts from this book which I believe are vitally relevant to many of the things that I have shared with you thus far.

Chapter 1:1, 3 begins; The **Book of the Prophet Ezra** ... from the tribe of Levi who was a captive in the country of the Medes in the reign of Artaxerxes, king of the Persians.

1:4, 5, 6, 8; The word of Ehyeh came to me saying, go and declare to my people their evil deeds and to their children the iniquities that they have committed against Me, so that they may tell their grandchildren that the sins of their parents have increased in them, <u>for they have forgotten me</u> and <u>have offered sacrifices, (slaughtered animals) to strange gods</u> ... <u>they have not obeyed my laws.</u>

1:24, 25; What shall I do to you, O Yacob? You, Yahuda, <u>would not obey me</u>. I will turn to other nations, and I will give them <u>my name</u> so that they may <u>keep my statutes. Because you have forsaken me, I will forsake you.</u>

1:31; When you offer oblations to me, I will turn my face from you, because **I have rejected your feast days and your new moons and circumcisions of the flesh**.

1:33; Thus says Ehyeh Almighty: Your house (family) is desolate.

2:7; Let them be scattered among the (heathen) nations; let their names be blotted out from the earth, because they have despised my covenant.

2:34, 38, 45; I say to you, O nations that hear and understand... Rise, stand erect, (upright) and see the number (144,000) who have been sealed at the feasts (Moeds) of Ehyeh... These are they who have put off mortal clothing and have put on immortal and have confessed the name of Ehyeh.

3:36; **You may indeed find individuals who have kept your commandments, but nations you will not find.**

5:23-27; I said, O Sovereign Ehyeh, from every forest of the earth and from all its trees you have chosen one vine. And from all the lands of the world you have chosen for yourself one region. And for all the flowers of the world you have chosen for yourself one lily. And from all the depths of the sea you have filled for yourself one river. And from all the cities that have been built you have consecrated Zion for yourself. And from all the birds that have been created you have named for yourself one dove. And from all the flocks that have been made you have provided for yourself one sheep. And from all the multitude of peoples you have gotten for yourself one people. And to this people (Yeshurun / the Upright) whom you have loved, you have given the law that is approved by all.

7:1-9; When I had finished speaking these words, the Malakim (4:1; **Uriel**) who had been sent to me on the former nights was sent to me again. He said to me, Rise,

Let Me Count The Ways In Which We Have All Been Deceived

Ezra and listen to the words that I have come to speak to you.

I said, Speak, my master. And he said to me, **there is a sea set in a wide expanse so that it is deep and vast, but it has an entrance set in a <u>narrow place</u> so that it is like a river**. If there are those who wish to reach the sea, to look at it or to navigate it, how can they come to the broad part unless they pass through the <u>narrow part</u>. Another example: There is a city built in a plain and it is full of goodly things. But the entrance to <u>it is narrow</u> and set in a precipitous place, so that there is fire on the right hand and deep water on the left. There is only one path lying between them, that is, between the fire and the water, so that only one person can walk on the path. If now the city is given to someone as an inheritance, how will the heir receive the inheritance unless by passing through the appointed danger? I said, that is right, master. He said to me, So also is Yeshurun's portion.

7:60, 61; ...I will <u>rejoice over the few who shall be saved</u>, because it is they who have made my majesty to prevail now and <u>through them my name has now been honored</u>. I will not grieve over the great number of those who perish; for it is they who are now like a mist and are similar to a flame and smoke - they are set on fire and burn hotly and are extinguished.

7:132, 133; I answered and said, I know, O master, the Most High is now called merciful, because he has mercy on those who have not yet come into the world; and gracious, because <u>he is gracious to those who turn (teshuva) in repentance to his law</u>.

8:1; He (Uriel) answered me and said, the Most High made this world for the sake of many, but <u>the world to come is for the sake of only a few</u>.

9:20-22; ...I considered my world and saw that it was lost. I saw that my earth was in peril because of the devices of those who had come into it. **And I saw and spared some with great difficulty and saved for myself <u>one grape out of a cluster and one plant out of a forest</u>. So, let the multitude that has been born in vain, perish; but <u>let my grape and my plant be saved</u>.**

14:34; If you will <u>rule over your minds and discipline your hearts</u>, you shall be kept alive and after death you shall obtain mercy.

16:54-56; Ehyeh certainly knows everything that people do. He knows their imaginations and their thoughts and their hearts. Ehyeh said, let the earth be made and it was made and let the heaven be made and it was made. At His word (command) <u>the stars were fixed in their places,</u> and He knows the number of the stars.

34
The Final Nail

I am fairly sure that you have heard the expression, "There is an elephant in the room." It is an idiom for an obvious truth that is either being completely ignored or it is being unaddressed. I have shared quite a few things with you that we have all been deceived about thus far. There are just too many to count. However, I want to make sure that you understand what it takes to be accounted as Yeshurun.

We discovered that the oracles or wise counsel of Ehyeh were committed to the Yahudians. We also learned is that Yeshua was born from the seed of David, which means that he was a Yahudian. **Revelation 14:12** says, *"Here is the patience of the saints: here are they that keep the commandments of Ehyeh and the faith of Yeshua."*

So, what is the faith of Yeshua? What exactly are we supposed to believe about Yeshua?

Today, we have the same problem that the Yahudians had back in their day. They had false preachers and scribes and we have the same problem today.

All of the commandments, the ordinances, the statutes, the decrees, the covenants and the beliefs have all been changed by man.

Let Me Count The Ways In Which We Have All Been Deceived

The reality of the issue is that we are supposed to obey the "teachings" of Yeshua. That is what the "faith of Yeshua is. It is obedience to his teachings. It is <u>not</u> just by believing in him.

Back on page 70 I gave the definition for the word "Christ." However, I did not go into explaining where the word "Christian" originated from. I intentionally left that one out because the word has several meanings, depending upon how you look at it. Most modern-day definitions will tell you that a Christian is a follower of Christ.

You can see that this is a major problem when you realize that the apostles who were with Yeshua did not ever call him Christ. As I said before, they called him master or teacher. The word "Christ" is a Greek word. The apostles were not Greek.

We have already established that his name was not "Jesus." His name was Yeshua. He was called the Messiah which was, "the deliverer." Yeshua was sent to teach the people the correct way to live and worship the Creator. However, in the end, there were very few righteous individuals who actually followed his true teachings.

Those who continued to follow Yeshua's teachings after he was killed and resurrected were scorned and ridiculed. The label that they were given was considered an insult. They were called "Cretins." According to the ***Urban Dictionary***, a "cretin" is "a person that is brainless, stupid, and child-like." A cretin was someone who was considered to be a fool.

This was the title that was given to those who followed Yeshua's teachings. You have to remember that Yeshua was killed because of what he was teaching. It was the High Priests who were ultimately behind his death. Overtime the title of "cretin" eventually turned into the title of "Christian." The title of Christian was originally considered to be an insult.

The scribes have manipulated and changed everything that Yeshua came for and taught.

The first of the seven commandments in **Exodus 34** tells us to take heed and not to make a covenant with the inhabitants of the land ... *"And thou take of their daughters unto thy sons and their daughters go a whoring after their gods and make thy sons go a whoring after their gods."*

The problem is that this has already happened many, many years ago. **Jude 1:6** says, *"The angels which kept not their first estate, but left their own habitations".* In the **Book of Yubilees 4:15** it says, *"And they called his name Jared, because the sons of Ehyeh descended from the mountain in his days, those who are called the Watchers, so that they would instruct the children of men so that they should do justice and righteousness on the earth."*

It was the righteous descendents of Seth who descended down from their set apart mountain during the time of Jared, who took and married the heathen descendant daughters of Cain. It was not angels as we have been falsely taught. The children of Seth were not supposed to defile themselves with the children of Cain. The name, "Jared" means, "descend."

As I have implied, our forefathers have already married into the pagan practices of the false worship of the other pagan deities. And as **Yeremiah 16:19** implies that: *"We have all inherited lies."*

Now we have to do as **Revelation 18:4** tells us and *"Come out of her my people."* We must learn what it means to, "Come out of the false confusing teachings of Babylon.

Let Me Count The Ways In Which We Have All Been Deceived

35
Index Of Words From Pagan Origins

- Monday - Moon
- Tuesday - Tyr
- Wednesday – Odin
- Thursday – Thor
- Friday – Frig
- Saturday – Saturn
- Sunday – Sun
- January – Janis
- February – Februa
- March – Mars
- April – Aphrodite
- May – Maia
- June – Juno
- July – Julius Cesar
- Amen – Amein

Let Me Count The Ways In Which We Have All Been Deceived

- Angel – Malakim
- Bible – Biblos
- Church – Circus
- Christ – Christos
- Glory - Gloria
- Holy – Holi
- Jesus – Zeus
- Jehovah – Yahweh
- Blessed – Sprinkled Blood
- Israel – Isis-Ra-El
- August – Augustus Caesar
- Sacrifice – Slaughter

36
Appendix

A List of Books That Were
Excluded From The Scriptures

A
Abraham, Book of
Abraham, Testament of
Acts of A King
Adam, The Book of
Adam, The Apocalypse of, (Revelation of)
Adam and Eve, Life of, the Greek Translation
Adam and Eve, The First Book of
Adam and Eve, The Second Book of
Adam and Eve, An Electronic Edition
Ages of The World, The
Archangel Michael And King Zedekiah, The

B
Book of The Bee, The
Book of Hymns, The

C
Chosen One, The
City of God, The
Creator, Hymn to the

Let Me Count The Ways In Which We Have All Been Deceived

D
Daniel and Susanna
Daniel, The Vision of
David, The Annals of King
David, Apocryphal Psalms of

E
Elijah, The Apocalypse of
Enoch (Ethiopic Apocalypse of Enoch)
Enoch, Secrets of
Enoch (Another Version)
Enoch And The Watchers
Giants, The Book of, (Attributed to Enoch)
Ephesians 2
Ezra, Fifth Book of
Ezra, Sixth Book of
Esdras, The Revelation of
Esther, The Remaining Chapters of
Eve, Gospel of
Exhortation Based On The Flood
Exodus
Ezekiel, Apocryphal of
Ezekiel the Tragedian
Ezra, Greek Apocalypse of
Ezra, Questions of
Ezra, Fourth Book of

F
Flavius Josephus

G
Genesis and Exodus, A Reworking of
Giants, The Book of, (Atttributed to Enoch)
Gilgamesh Epic, The Flood Narrative From the
Gospel of Truth

H
Hebrews, Gospel of (Hebrews 2)
Heresies, Against the
Hermas
Hesychius, False Gospels of the
Hosea Commentary

I
In Praise of Wisdom
Israel and the Holy Land

J
Jasher
Jubilees, Book of
Job, Testament of
Joseph the Carpenter, The History of
Judas Iscariot, Gospel of
Jude, Gospel of

K
Kings, The Third Book of
Kings, The Fourth Book of
Knowledge, The Interpretation of

L
Laodiceans, The Epistle to
Lucian of Samosata
Lucian of Samosata, Alexander the False Prophet

Lucian of Samosata, The Passing of Peregrinus
Lucianus, The False Gospels

M
Melchizedek
Melchizedek, The Coming of
Michael, Words of
Moses, Book of
Moses, The Sixth Book of
Moses, The Seventh Book of
Moses, The Revelation of
Moses, The Words of

N
Nazarenes, Gospel According to the

O
Ordinances
Origen
Origin of the World, On the

P
Parable of the Bountiful Tree, The
Patriarchs, Lives of The
Patriarchs, Tales of the
Polycrates of Ephesus
Polycarp, Martyrdom of
Priestly Service
Prophets, The Lives of the
Proverbs, A Collection of
Psalms, Commentary on
Psalms: Dead Sea Scroll

Let Me Count The Ways In Which We Have All Been Deceived

S
Secret of The Way Things Are, The
Secrets, The Book of
Seth, Revelation of Adam's Origin
Seth, The Second Treatise of the Great
Seth, The Three Steles of
Shem, The Paraphrase of
Shepherd of Hermas

T
Talmud
Acts of Thomas
Apocalypse of Thomas
Gospel of Thomas
Thomas, Secret Gospel
Three Patriarchs, Testaments of the
Treasures, The Cave of
Treatise on the Resurrection
Twelve Apostles, Gospel of
Twelve Patriarchs, Testaments of the
Two Ways, The

W
War Rule
Wars of the Jews
War Scroll, The
The Wisdom Text

Z
Fragments of a Zadokite Work

37
The Book Of Oahspe

Have you ever heard of the **Book of Oahspe**? I have just recently had an opportunity to read this book. It is a very profound book. I suggest that you get a copy and read it. The following is a set of excerpts from this **Book of Oahspe**.

From the Glossary; "Beast." is (1). the animal, man. And (2), it is; Anything that is enforced as a religion.

Genesis 2:10 says, "And a river went out of Eden to water the garden; and from thence it was parted and became into four heads.

Revelation 17:15 says, "And he saith unto me, the waters which thou saw, where the whore sits, are peoples and multitudes and nations and tongues.

11. The Beast divided itself into four great heads and possessed the earth; and man fell down and worshipped them.

12. The names of the heads of the Beast were, **BRAHMIN**, (which is) **HINDUISM, BUDDHIST, CHRISTIAN,** AND **MOHAMMEDAN**. And they divided the earth and apportioned it between themselves.

Let Me Count The Ways In Which We Have All Been Deceived

The following is from the: **Book of Ah'shong 7/3.18**: What is so conceited as man? And yet I bring him into life, the dumbest of animals. Man prides himself in his power and wisdom. But I send the drought, the rains and the winds, the weakest of my members and they show man that he is nothing.

The Voice Of Mankind

"O Ehyeh, what am I that I should pray to You? Do I even know my own weakness, or do I understand the way of my thoughts? You have placed before me most wonderful creations. They impress me, and my senses rise up in remembrance of the Almighty. Where have I invented even one thought other than by looking upon Your works? How can I do otherwise than remember my Creator and out of Your creations, O Ehyeh, find rich food for meditation all the days of my life?

And yet, though I have appropriated the earth to myself, I am neither happy nor perfect. Misery, crime and selfishness are upon my people.

What is my weakness that I cannot overcome it? Or what is my strength that I give in to the desires of the earth? I build up my belief and courage in You; but before I know the way of my weakness, I stumble and fall. Am I made that I shall be forever a disappointment to myself and a censure to my own behavior?

How can I say to anyone: Be pure and set-apart, O man! Are my flesh and blood not proof that man cannot be without sin? O this corruptible self, this tendency to fall from the right way! You, O my Creator, have proven to my senses, every day of my life, that You alone are mighty in purity and truth.

Let Me Count The Ways In Which We Have All Been Deceived

If only I had a starting point from which to estimate Your wonderful decrees or could find a road in which I would never stumble! But yet, O Ehyeh, I will not complain because of the way of Your works. You have established a limit to my understanding, by which I am reminded of You, to call upon Your name. I perceive my own vanity; that were all knowledge mine, I would become less beholden to You!

What am I, O Ehyeh, without You; or how am I to find the splendor of Your creations, other than by the light of Your countenance? You raised me up out of sin and darkness and clothed me in light. I perceive the smallness of myself in Your great works. You have bound me to travel on the earth, to sojourn with beasts and all types of creeping things; nor have You given me one attribute in which I can boast over them, except in the power of destruction. The high firmament You have placed above me, the stars, moon and sun! I know You have been there, but I am bound down in a little corner of Your works! Neither do I have power to rise up to Your distant places, nor to know and understand Your extended heavens.

No, I do not even have power to shape my own size and stature; but all things take form and dimension whether I will it or not. In Your own way the walls of the world are built; by their magnitude I am confounded; by the majesty of Your hand, appalled. Why have I vainly set myself up as the highest of Your works? My failures are worse than any other living creature under the sun. I cannot build my house in perfection as a bird does; my ingenuity cannot fashion a spider's net; I cannot sail up in the air like a bird, nor live in the water like the fish, nor dwell in harmony like the bee. Half of my offspring die in infancy; and the multitude of my household are quarrelers, fighters, drunkards and beggars; the best of my sons and daughters are less faithful than a dog! I go forth to war, to slay my brothers, even while Your wide earth has room for all of us. Yes, I plague the earth with starvation, sin and untimely death. O, if only I could educate myself to not boast of my own greatness; instead I should be forever ashamed in Your sight, O Ehyeh!

But I will acknowledge my iniquities; I can hide nothing from the eye of my Creator. Hear me then, O Father!

I took up arms against my brother. With great armies I encompassed him, to desecrate him.

By the stroke of my sword I multiplied his widows and orphans; the cry of anguish that came out of their mouths I answered by the destruction of my brother's harvests.

I built monuments in stone and iron to my captains and generals who showed great skill in killing. Yes, I inscribed them from top to bottom with their bloody victories.

And in my vanity I called out to the young, saying; Behold the grandeur of these great men! I have built these great monuments to honor them!

And the youth of my household were whetted with ambition for destruction. The example of my hand made them train themselves for warfare.

To my colonels and generals, I gave badges of gold. I called to the young women, saying; Come, a great honor I give you; you shall dance with the officers of death!

And they fluttered up on tip-toe, elated by the honey of my words! O Ehyeh, how wide open is my wickedness; how utterly I have failed, except in making the flow of my brother's blood the relish of satan!

Let Me Count The Ways In Which We Have All Been Deceived

To my destroying hosts I have given great honor and splendor. In the pretense of enforcing peace, I hewed my way in flesh and blood.

I made an illusion, a kingdom. I called out to my people, saying; We must have a kingdom! I showed them no reason for it; but I pressed them to take up arms and follow me for patriotism's sake. And yet what was patriotism? Behold, I made it as something greater than You and Your commandment: **YOU SHALL NOT KILL**.

Yes, by the cunning of my words, I taught them my brother was my enemy; that to fall upon and destroy him and his people was great patriotism.

And they ran at the sound of my voice, for my credit in the greatness of my kingdom; and they committed great devastation.

Yes, I built colleges for training my young men in warfare. I drew boundaries, making borders here and there, saying; This is my kingdom! All others are my enemies!

I patted my young men on the head, saying; You dogs of war! Great shall be your fame!

And their judgment was turned away from peace; I made them think that righteousness was to stand up for me and my country and to destroy my brother and his people.

Yes, they built me forts, castles and arsenals, without number. I called to my people, saying; Come, behold the splendor of my defenses which I built for you!

And they gave me money, garrisons, ships of war and torpedoes, shouting: Hurrah for our kingdom! We have faith in these things, but not in You, our Creator!

Let Me Count The Ways In Which We Have All Been Deceived

Thus I led them away from You. Their eyes I turned to look down, in the way of death. By the might of my armies, I put away righteousness.

Yes, I covered the earth over with drunkards, widows and orphans; I reduced them to beggary; but I whetted their pride by saying; Look what great standing armies we have!

To the man who said: There shall come a time of peace, when war shall be no more forever, I mocked and said: You fool!

O Father, I know the counts against me. I cannot hide my iniquity from Your sight. I have said war was a necessary evil to prevent a too populous world! I turned my back on the wide, unsettled regions of the earth. With this falsehood in my mouth I stood up before You! Yes, I cried out as if for the righteous, saying; I war for righteousness and for the protection of the weak! In the destruction of my brothers and sisters I stood as a murderer, pleading this excuse. Stubbornly I persisted in not seeing justice on the other side, while I cut down those whom You had created alive. Above the works of Your hand, I raised myself up as a pruning knife in Your vineyard.

Even more than this, I persuaded my sons and daughters that to war for me was to war for our Father in heaven. By my blasphemy I led them into ruin. And when the battle was over for a day, I cried out: Behold the wonder of those who were slain for the honor of their country! Thus I have added crime to crime before You, Ehyeh; and so, destroyed Your beautiful creation. Truly, I have not one word in justification of my deeds before You!

O, if only I had remained faithful with You, Ehyeh! But I made-up gods to the credit of the evil one. In one place I called out to my sons and daughters, saying; Be **Brahmins**; <u>Brahma saves whoever professes his name</u>. In

Let Me Count The Ways In Which We Have All Been Deceived

another place I said: Be **Buddhists**; <u>Buddha saves whoever calls on his name</u>. In another place I said: Be **Christians**; <u>Christ saves whoever calls on his name</u>. In another place I said: Be **Mohammedans**; whoever says, "<u>There is only one God and Mohammed is his prophet!</u>" shall have indulgence without sin.

Thus I have divided the earth, O Ehyeh! I have established them <u>into four great idolatries</u> and into their hands put all manner of weapons of destruction; and they have become more terrible against one another than the beasts of the forest. O, if only I could put away these great iniquities which I raised up as everlasting torments to the earth. Truly, there is no salvation in any of these.

Their people are continually destroying one another. They quarrel and kill for their respective religions; Setting aside Your commandment: You shall not kill. They love their own nation and hate all others. They set aside Your commandment: Love your neighbor as yourself.

They preach and pray in sufficient truth; but not one of these people practices peace, love and virtue, in any degree equal to their understanding. These religions have not saved any nation or city on the whole earth from sin.

In vain I have searched for a plan of redemption; a plan that would make the earth a paradise and the life of man a credit to You our Creator and a joy to himself. But alas, the two extremes, riches and poverty, have made the prospect of a millennium a thing of mockery.

For one rich man there are a thousand poor and their interests ceaselessly conflict with one another. Labor cries out in pain; but capital strikes him with a heartless blow.

Let Me Count The Ways In Which We Have All Been Deceived

Nation is against nation; king against king; merchant against merchant; consumer against producer; yes, man against man, in all things upon the earth.

Because the state is rotten, the politician feeds on it; because society is rotten, the lawyer and court have riches and sumptuous feasts; because the flesh of my people is rotten, the physician finds a harvest of comfort.

Now, O Ehyeh, I come to You! You hold the secret of peace, harmony and goodwill among mortals. Give me of Your light, O Father! Show me the way to proceed so that war, crime and poverty, may come to an end. Open the way of peace, love, virtue and truth, so that Your children may rejoice in their lives and magnify You and Your works forever.

Such is the voice of man, O Ehyeh! In all the nations of the earth this voice rises up to You! Just as You spoke to Zarathustra, Abraham and Moses, leading them forth out of darkness, O Ehyeh speak!

`Man has faith in You only; You alone were sufficient for the past: You alone are sufficient for Your own creation today. O Ehyeh Speak"!

38
The Conclusion

Mankind had been deceived on practically every conceivable level. After the flood, Ehyeh commanded the people to disperse throughout the earth and multiply. However, the people were afraid that there would be another flood, so they began building a tower to heaven. As it began to get bigger and bigger Ehyeh took notice. It was at this time that Ehyeh went down and confused the people's languages.

Up until this time the tower was not called the "Tower Of Babble". It was only called the Tower of Babble after Ehyeh changed the people's languages. It is my personal belief that Ehyeh did not just change the people's language from one language to another, but I believe that he made it so that even those of the same language could not completely understand each other.

For instance, the word "eat" has several meanings in the English language. It could mean; *to eat, to consume or burn.* So, what happens is when we translate words from one language to another, we can also mistranslate the meaning of the original intent.

Psalms 1:1-3 says, "Favored *is* the person that does not walk in the counsel of the ungodly, nor stands in the path of <u>sinners</u>, nor <u>sits</u> in the seat of the scornful. 2 For his delight *is* in the instruction of Ehyeh; and in His instruction does he meditate day and night. 3 He shall be like a tree planted by the rivers of water, that brings forth his fruit in his season; his leaf also shall not wither; and whatsoever he does shall prosper".

Scripture alludes to the fact that Ehyeh is the potter who makes the pot from the clay (earth). If we are the plants / trees that go into the pots that Ehyeh has made, then we are reckoned as vegetation. This way when we consume fruits and vegetables, we are in fact burning incense and when we pray to Ehyeh we are praying with a pure and clean heart from a clean vessel.

Psalms 19:1-6 says, "The heavens declare the majesty of Ehyeh; and the firmament shows His handy work. 2 Day after day it utters speech, and night unto night it reveals knowledge. 3 *There is* no sound nor language *where* their voice is not heard. 4 Their line is gone through out all the earth, and their words to the end of the world. In out them has he set a <u>tabernacle</u> for the sun, 5 Which *is* as a bridegroom coming out of his chamber, *who* rejoices as a strong man to run a race. 6 His going forth *is* from the end of the heaven, and his circuit goes unto the ends of it: and there is nothing hid from the heat thereof".

Ehyeh set four separate <u>tabernacles</u> in the heaven for the sun to travel through. These tabernacles are the four quarterly seasons. We have been instructed to observe these four tabernacles of Ehyeh "on earth as it is in heaven".

We have also been instructed to come before Ehyeh three times a year. What if, we are actually supposed to appear before Ehyeh (three times a day)?

Let Me Count The Ways In Which We Have All Been Deceived

Scripture mentions the "Abomination of Desolation" spoken of by Daniel the prophet. Daniel was a vegetarian. Daniel was given ten times the wisdom because he was a vegetarian. He was also thrown into the lion's den because he refused to quit praying to Ehyeh three times a day.

Could it be possible that this is the "Will of the father in heaven"?

Is this what it means to "Come out of Babylon"? **Isaiah 66:20** says, And they shall bring all your brethren *for* an offering unto Ehyeh out of all nations upon horses, and in chariots, and in litters, and upon mules, and upon swift beasts, to my set-apart mountain Jerusalem, saith Ehyeh, as the children of Yeshurun bring an offering in a clean vessel into the house of Ehyeh.

Let Me Count The Ways In Which We Have All Been Deceived

39
From The Author

I wrote this book for the people of Yeshurun, (The Upright) who are striving to search and discover the original truth. I would be willing to believe that more than half of those individuals who have gotten frustrated and completely quit going to their various assemblies have simply quit going because they know for a certainty that what they have been taught is not The Truth. The problem is that they do not know where to go in order to find The Truth that they are looking for.

This book was not written as a tell all. There is still a lot more truth to be discovered and understood by those of you who will take what you have learned here and build upon it.

I was pretty general in some of the things which I have shared with you. There are a lot more specifics that you can glean from your own pages of Scripture and all of these other unique books that I have told you about, now that you have an idea what to look for.

There was a time when I did not know any of this truth either. As I like to tell people, "you cannot learn anything new if you do not hear about it or read about it first." I personally believe that a person cannot teach any of this to someone else if they are not practicing it themselves.

I believe in everything that I have shared with you in this book. You, (the reader) on the other hand can choose to believe all of it or none of it as you please. If you want to, you can also choose to believe just parts of it. **Deuteronomy 30:19** tells us, "...*I have set before you life and death, favorings and cursing: Therefore choose life, so that both you and your children may live*":

Do you recall what I told you at the beginning? I said that knowledge is a two-edged sword. Now that you have read this book, you are now responsible for the knowledge that you now have. I pray that you have had an opportunity to have a "renewing of your mind." Now you can only move forward from here.

I would appreciate it if you would be kind enough to recommend this book to anyone you know of who is seriously searching for "**The Truth**."

Boyd B. McNiel

Please check out my five other books that I have published.

The things which I have shared with you in this book are just the tip of the iceberg when it concerns the things which we have all been deceived about. If I have piqued your curiosity at all, you will want to get my five other books which are titled:

- **The Investigative Interpretation Of The Book of Yubilees**
- **Armageddon The Mystery Unveiled**
- **Knowledge Of The Truth Verses World-Wide Deception**
- **My People Are Destroyed For Lack Of Knowledge**
- **World-Wide Deception Exposed**

Let Me Count The Ways In Which We Have All Been Deceived

ARMAGEDDON
THE MYSTERY UNVEILED

Boyd B. McNiel

The
Investigative Interpretation
of the
Book of Jubilees

⚜

Dividing the Light from the Darkness

⚜

Boyd B. McNiel

Remember!

Your preachers cannot and will not tell you the things that they do not know for themselves.

Let Me Count The Ways In Which We Have All Been Deceived

Woe Unto You, Scribes And Pharisees, You hypocrites!

Scripture explicitly tells us, "If *it were* possible, they, (the Scribes and the Pharisees) shall deceive the very elect." Scripture goes on to say that "The pen of the scribes is in vain" and that "Our fathers have inherited lies."

Discover what Scripture means when it says:

- **But of the times and the seasons.**
- **They have transgressed the laws.**
- **They have changed the ordinances.**
- **They have broken the everlasting covenant.**

Are you one of those individuals who knows that your preacher is not telling you the entire story? If so, then this book is for you. Your preachers can not and will not tell you the things that they do not know for themselves.

Boyd B. McNiel

Made in the USA
Middletown, DE
21 September 2022